Maximilia

A Woman's Reminiscences of the French Intervention 1862-1867

Sara Yorke Stevenson

Alpha Editions

This edition published in 2022

ISBN : 9789356896451

Design and Setting By
Alpha Editions
www.alphaedis.com
Email - info@alphaedis.com

Contents

PRELUDE

In offering these pages to the public, my aim is not to write a historical sketch of the reign of Maximilian of Austria, nor is it to give a description of the political crisis through which Mexico passed during that period. My only desire is to furnish the reader with a point of view the value of which lies in the fact that it is that of an eyewitness who was somewhat more than an ordinary spectator of a series of occurrences which developed into one of the most dramatic episodes of modern times.

Historians too often present their personages to the public and to posterity as actors upon a stage,—I was about to say as puppets in a show,—whose acts are quite outside of themselves, and whose voices express emotions not their own. They appear before the footlights of a fulfilled destiny; and their doubts, their weaknesses, are concealed, along with their temptations, beneath the paint and stage drapery lent them by the historian who, knowing beforehand the denouement toward which their efforts tended, unconsciously assumes a like knowledge on their part. They are thus often credited with deep-laid motives and plans which it may perhaps have been impossible for them to entertain at the time.

To those who lived with them when they were MAKING history, these actors are all aglow with life. They are animated by its passions, its impulses. They are urged onward by personal ambition, or held back by selfish considerations. They are not characters in a drama; they are men of the world, whose official acts, like those of the men about us to-day, are influenced by their affections, their family complications, their prejudices, their rivalries, their avarice, their vanity. The circumstances of their private life temporarily excite or depress their energies, and often give them a new and unlooked-for direction; and the success or failure of their undertakings may be recognized as having been the result of their individual limitations, of their personal ignorance of the special conditions with which they were called upon to cope, or of their short-sightedness.

In this lies the importance of private recollections. The gossip of one epoch forms part of the history of the next. It is therefore to be deplored that those whose more or less obscure lives run their course in the shadow of some public career are seldom sufficiently aware of the fact at the time to note accurately their observations and impressions.

These thoughts occurred to me when, at the request of the editor of the "Century," I one night took up my pen, and gathering about me old letters, photographs, and small tokens faded and yellow with age, plunged deep into the recollections of my youthful days, and evoked the ghosts of brilliant friends, many of whom have since passed away, leaving but names written in lines of blood upon a page of history. As they appeared across a chasm of thirty years, the well-remembered faces familiarly smiled, each flinging a memory. They formed a motley company: generals now dead, whose names are revered or execrated by their countrymen; lieutenants and captains who have since made their way in the world, or have died, broken-hearted heroes, before Metz or Sedan; women who seemed obscure, but whose names, in the general convulsion of nations, have risen to newspaper notoriety or to lasting fame; soldiers who have become historians; guerrilleros now pompously called generals; adventurers who have grown into personages; personages who have sunk into adventurers; sovereigns who have become martyrs.

They had all been laid away in my mind, buried in the ashes of the past along with the old life. The drama in which each had played his part had for many years seemed as far off and dim as though read in a book a long time ago; and yet now, how alive it all suddenly became—alive with a life that no pen can picture!

There were their photographs and their invitations, their old notes and bits of doggerel sent to accompany small courtesies—flowers, music, a Havana dog, or the loan of a horse. It was all vivid and real enough now. Those men were not to me mere historical figures of whom one reads. They fought historic battles, they founded a historic though ephemeral empire; their defeats, their triumphs, their "deals," their blunders, were now matters of history: but for all that, they were of common flesh and blood, and the strange incidents of a strangely picturesque episode in the existence of this continent seemed natural enough if one only knew the men.

Singly or in groups, the procession slowly passed, each one pausing for a brief space in the flood of light cast by an awakening memory. Many wore uniforms—French, Austrian, Belgian, Mexican. Some were dancing gaily, laughing and flirting as they went by. Others looked careworn and absorbed by the preoccupations of a distracted state, and by the growing consciousness of the thankless responsibility which the incapacity of their rulers at home, and the unprincipled deceit of a few official impostors, had placed upon them. But all, whether thoughtful or careless, whether clairvoyant or blind, whether calmly yielding to fate or attempting to breast the storm, were driven along by the irresistible current of events, each drifting toward the darkness of an inevitable doom which, we now know, was inexorably awaiting him as he passed from the ray of light into the gloom in his "dance to death."

PART I.

THE TRIPLE ALLIANCE

1861-62

MAXIMILIAN IN MEXICO

I. EL DORADO

During the winter of 1861-62, my last winter in France, one of the principal subjects of conversation in Parisian official circles was our Civil War, and its possible bearing upon the commercial and colonial interests of Europe, or rather the possible advantage that Europe, and especially France, might hope to derive from it.

A glance at M. de Lamartine's famous article written in January, 1864, and reprinted a year or two later in his "Entretiens Litteraires," will help us to understand how far Frenchmen were from appreciating not only our point of view, but the true place assigned by fate to the United States in contemporary history. Nothing could so plainly reveal the failure of the French to understand the natural drift of events on this side of the Atlantic, and account for the extraordinary, though shortlived, success of Napoleon's wild Mexican scheme. In this article, written with a servile pen, the poet-statesman attacked the character of the people of the United States, and brought out Napoleon's motives in his attempt to obtain, not for France alone, but for Europe at large, a foothold upon the American continent. With a vividness likely to impress his readers with the greatness of the conception as a theory, he showed how the establishment of a European monarchy in Mexico must insure to European nations a share in the commerce of the New World. The new continent, America, is the property of Europe, he urged. The Old World should not recognize the right of the United States to control its wealth and power.

An article by Michel Chevalier, published with the same purpose in view, threatened Mexico with annexation by the United States unless the existing government of the country underwent reorganization.

Both authors were frequent visitors at my guardian's house in Paris, which accounts for the impression made upon my youthful mind by their written utterances at that time. M. Chevalier was a distinguished political economist. He had visited Mexico, and knew the value of its mining and agricultural wealth without sufficiently recognizing the actual conditions to be dealt with, and he fully indorsed the imperial conception. "The success of the expedition is infallible," he said. He explained the resistance of the Mexicans by their hatred of the Spaniards, and demonstrated to his own satisfaction that the burden of the venture must fall upon France, who should reap the glory of its success.

Modern civilization, he urged, includes a distinct branch—the Latin—in which Catholicism shines. Of this France is the soul as well as the arm. "Without her, without her energy and her initiative the group of the Latin races must be reduced to a subordinate rank in the world, and would have been eclipsed long ago." In comparing upon a map of the world the space occupied by the Catholic nations two centuries ago with the present area under their control, "one is dismayed at all that they have lost and are losing" every day. "The Catholic nations seem threatened to be swallowed up by an ever-rising flood."*

* "Revue des Deux Mondes," of April, 1862, p. 916. It is interesting to find him quoting Humboldt's prophecy that "the time will come, be it a century sooner or later, when the production of silver will have no other limit than that imposed upon it by its ever-increasing depreciation as a value." (April, 1862, p. 894).

When the Mexican empire was planned our Civil War had been raging for nearly two years. From the standpoint of the French rulers, the moment seemed auspicious for France to interfere in American affairs. The establishment of a great Latin empire, founded under French protection and developed in the interest of France, which must necessarily derive the principal benefit of the stupendous wealth which Mexico held ready to pour into the lap of French capitalists,—of an empire which in the West might put a limit to the supremacy of the United States, as well as counterbalance the British supremacy in the East, thus opposing a formidable check to the encroachments of the Anglo-Saxon race in the interest of the Latin nations,—such was Napoleon's plan, and I have been told by one who was close to the imperial family at that time that the Emperor himself fondly regarded it as "the conception of his reign."

Napoleon III labored under the disadvantage of reigning beneath the shadow of a great personality which, consciously or unconsciously, he ever strove to emulate. But however clever he may be, the man who, anxious to appear or even to be great, forces fate and creates impossible situations that he may act a leading part before the world, is only a schemer. This is the key to the character of Napoleon III and to his failures. He looked far away and dreamed of universal achievements, when at home, at his very door, were the threatening issues he should have mastered. The story is told of him that one evening, at the Tuileries, when the imperial party were playing games, chance brought to the Emperor the question, "What is your favorite occupation?" to which he answered: "To seek the solution of unsolvable problems." It is also related that in his younger days a favorite axiom of his was: "Follow the ideas of your time, they carry you along; struggle against them, they overcome you; precede them, they support you." True enough; but only upon condition that you will not mistake the shrill chorus of a few interested courtiers and speculators for the voice of your time, nor imagine that you precede your generation because you stand alone. He dreamed of far-away glory, and his flatterers told him his dreams were prophetic. He saw across the seas the mirage of a great Latin empire in the West, and beheld the Muse of history inscribing his name beside that of his great kinsman as the restorer of the political and commercial equilibrium of the world, as well as the benefactor who had thrown El Dorado open to civilization. With the faith of ignorance, he proposed to share with an Austrian archduke these imaginary possessions, and to lay for him, as was popularly said in 1862-63, "a bed of roses in a gold-mine." Unmindful of warnings, he pushed onward for two years, apparently incapable of grasping the fact that the mirage was receding before him; and finally found his fool's errand saved from ridicule only by the holocaust of many lives, and raised to dignity only by the tragedy of Queretaro.

All this we now know, but in 1861-62 the Napoleonic star shone brilliantly with the full luster cast upon it by the Crimean war and the result of the Italian campaign. It is true that occasionally some strong discordant note issuing from the popular depths would strike the ear and for the time mar the paeans of applause which always greet successful power. For instance, at the Odeon one night, during the war with Austria, I was present when the Empress Eugenie entered. The Odeon is in the Latin Quarter, and medical and law students filled the upper tiers of the house. As the sovereign took her seat in a box a mighty chorus suddenly arose, and hundreds of voices sang, "Corbleu, madame, que faites vous ici?" quoting the then popular song, "Le Sire de Franboisy."

The incident, so insulting to the poor woman, gave rise to some disturbance; and although the boys were quieted, the Empress soon left the theater, choking with mortification. M. Rochefort, who refers to this incident in his memoirs, adds that as the imperial party came out, another insult of a still more shocking character was thrown at the Empress. This, of course, I did not witness.

Such occurrences were usually treated by the press and the government sympathizers as emanating from youthful hot-brains, or from the lower ranks of the people, and therefore as unworthy of attention. But those hot-brains represented the coming thinkers of France, and the "common" people represented its strength. On the whole, however, in 1862 the more powerful element had rallied to and upheld the government. The court and the army were so loud in their admiration of the profound policy of the Emperor that those who heeded the croakings of the few clear-sighted men composing the opposition were in the background.

It so happened that my lines had been cast among these, and it is interesting now, in looking back upon the expressions of opinion of those who most strenuously opposed French interference in American affairs, to see how little even these men, wise as they were in their generation, appreciated the true conditions prevailing in Mexico. None seriously doubted the possibility of occupying the country and of maintaining a French protectorate. The only point discussed was, Was it worth while? And to this question Jules Favre, Thiers, Picard, Berryer, Glais-Bizoin, Pelletan, and a few others emphatically said, "No!"

II. THE NEW "NAPOLEONIC IDEA"

The "Napoleonic idea," however, had not burst forth fully equipped in all its details from the Caesarean brain in 1862. It would be unfair not to allow it worthy antecedents and a place in the historic sequence. As far back as 1821, when the principle of constitutional monarchy was accepted by the Mexicans under the influence of General Iturbide, a convention known as the "plan of Iguala" had been drawn by Generals Iturbide and Santa Anna, and accepted by the new viceroy, O'Donoju, in which it was agreed that the crown of Mexico should be offered first to Ferdinand VII, and, in case of his refusal, to the Archduke Charles of Austria, or to the Infante of Spain, Don Carlos Luis, or to Don Francisco Paulo.

The Mexican embassy sent to Spain to offer the throne of Mexico to Ferdinand was ill received. The king had no thought of purchasing a crown which he regarded as his own by the recognition of the constitutional principle which he had so long fought; and the Cortes scorned to authorize any of the Spanish princes to accept the advances of the Mexicans. The result of Spain's unbending policy was a rupture which involved the loss of its richest colony.

In 1854 General Santa Anna,* then dictator or president for life, had given full powers to Senor Gutierrez de Estrada to treat with the courts of Paris, London, Vienna, and Madrid for the establishment of a monarchy in Mexico under the scepter of a European prince; and Senor de Estrada, with the consent of the French government, had offered the throne of his country to the Duc de Montpensier, who wisely, as it proved, had declined it.

* Santa Anna raised the flag of revolt against his benefactor in 1823. Iturbide abdicated, was given a pension of twenty-five thousand dollars, and, at his own suggestion, was escorted to the sea-coast, a voluntary exile, by a guard of honor. From this time Santa Anna had a hand in all the revolutions that followed. He himself subsequently fell before an insurrection of the Liberal party led by the old Indian governor of Guerrero, General Alvarez.

The Crimean war and the downfall of General Santa Anna checked the progress of these negotiations, which were resumed as soon as, peace having been restored, the European powers could turn their attention to their commercial interests in America, which Senor de Estrada represented to them as gravely compromised by the encroachments of the United States in Mexico, and to the grievances urged by their subjects against the Mexican government.*

* Compare Abbe Domenech, "Histoire du Mexique," vol. ii, p. 360.

In 1859 General Miramon* confirmed the powers given by General Santa Anna to the Mexican representative; and then it was that, for the first time, the Emperor commended to his attention the Archduke Maximilian.

* General Miramon was barely twenty-six when he rose to the first rank in Mexican politics. Of Bearnese extraction, his father's family passed over to Spain in the eighteenth century. His grandfather had gone to Mexico as aide de-camp to one of the viceroys. Miguel Miramon had served in the war against the United States. He was a brilliant officer, bold, vigorous, original. During his term of office he had on his side the clergy, the army, the capital.

It were also unfair not to admit that the varying success of the conflict between the two factions struggling for supremacy in Mexico was likely to deceive the European powers, and made it easy for men whose personal interests were at stake to misrepresent the respective strength of the contending parties and the condition of the country. But no leader of men has, in the eyes of history, a right to be deceived either by men or by appearances; and granting that Napoleon might at first have been misled, he had timely warning, and the opportunity to withdraw, as did the Spaniards and the English, without shame, if without glory.

After Mexico, led by the patriots Hidalgo and Morelos, had thrown off the Spanish yoke, it became for forty years the scene of a series of struggles between contending factions which reduced the country to a state of anarchy. Once rid of their Spanish viceroys, the Mexicans found themselves little better off than they had been under their rule. For centuries the Mexican church had played upon the piety of the devout for the furtherance of its own temporal interests, until one third of the whole wealth of the nation had found its way into its hands. It was against the clergy, and against the retrogressive policy for which it stood, that in 1856 a wide-spread revolutionary movement was successfully organized, as a result of which, in 1857, a liberal constitution was drawn up and accepted by the people.

The clerical or reactionary party, although it counted among its adherents many of the best old Spanish families composing Mexico's aristocracy, would probably soon have ceased to be a serious practical obstacle in the way of reform had it not been for the wealth of a corrupt clergy, by means of which its armies were kept in the field. Be this as it may, the reign of constitutional order represented by President Comonfort in 1856 was shortlived, General Comonfort abdicated in 1858. Benito Juarez, by virtue of his rank of president of the Supreme Court, then became constitutional president ad interim.

By a pronunciamiento General Zuloaga, with the help of the army, took possession of the government and of the capital, while Juarez maintained his rights at Queretaro. War raged between the two parties, with rapidly varying success. A letter dated November 19,1860, written by my brother, a young American engineer who had gone to Mexico to take part in the construction of the first piece of railroad built between Vera Cruz and Mexico, gives a concise and picturesque account of the situation:

Things look dark—so dark, in fact, that for the present I do not think it advisable to risk any more money here. There is a fair prospect of the decree of Juarez being annulled. If so, our bonds go overboard. There is a prospect of Juarez signing a treaty. If so, our bonds go up 15 or 20. It is rouge et noire—a throw of the dice. The Liberals have been beaten at Queretaro, where Miramon took from them twenty-one pieces of artillery and many prisoners, among them an American officer of artillery, whom he shot the next day, AS USUAL. Oajaca has fallen into the hands of the clergy. The Liberals under Carbajal attacked Tulancingo, and were disgracefully beaten by a lot of ragged Indians. They are losing ground everywhere; and if the United States does not take hold of this unhappy country it will certainly go to the dogs. There is a possibility of compromise between Juarez and Miramon, the effect of which is this: the constitution of '57 to be revised; the sale of clergy property to their profit; the revocation of Juarez's decree of July about the confiscation of clergy property to the profit of the state; religious liberty, civil marriage, etc.

A gloomy picture, and true enough, save in one respect. The Liberals might be beaten everywhere, but they were not losing ground; on the contrary, their cause rested upon too solid a foundation of right and progress, and the last brilliant exploits of General Miramon were insufficient to galvanize the reactionary party into a living force.

On December 22, 1860, Miramon was finally defeated at Calpulalpan by General Ortega, and shortly after left the country. On December 28 the reforms prepared in Vera Cruz by Juarez, proclaiming the principles of religious toleration, and decreeing the confiscation of clergy property, the abolition of all 13 religious orders, and the institution of civil marriage, etc., were promulgated in the capital by General Ortega; and on January 11,1861,

Juarez* himself took possession of the city of Mexico. The Liberals were triumphant, and the civil war was virtually at an end.

* Benito Pablo Juarez was of Indian birth, and as a boy began life as a mozo, or servant, in a wealthy family. His ability was such as to draw upon him the attention of his employer, who had him educated. He soon rose to greatness as a lawyer, and then as a member of the National Congress, governor of Oajaca, secretary to the executive, and president of the republic.

The defeated army, as was invariably the case in Mexico, dissolved and disappeared, leaving only a residuum of small bands of guerrillas. These preyed impartially upon the people and upon travelers of both parties. Leonardo Marquez almost alone remained in the field and seriously continued the conflict. The principal leaders fled abroad, especially to Paris, where they made friends, and planned a revenge upon the victorious oppressors of the church, whose outrages upon God and man were vividly colored by religious and party hatred. Among these were men of refinement and good address, scions of old Spanish families, who, like M. Gutierrez de Estrada, found ready sympathy among the Emperor's entourage. As a rule, none but "hopelessly defeated parties seek the help of foreign invasion of their own land"; but the Empress Eugenie, who, a Spaniard herself, was a devout churchwoman, lent a willing ear to the stories of the refugees, impressively told in her own native tongue. To reinstate the church, and to oppose the strong Catholicism of a Latin monarchy to the Protestant influence of the Northern republic, seemed to her the most attractive aspect of the projected scheme.

The struggle that had been carried on for so many years in Mexico with varying vicissitudes was not purely one of partizan interest based upon a different view of political government: it was the struggle of the spirit of the nineteenth century against the survival of Spanish medievalism; it was the contest of American republicanism against the old order of things, religious and social as well as political; of progressive liberalism against conservatism and reaction.

The French intervention as planned by Napoleon III was, therefore, a glaring paradox, and betrays his absolute ignorance of the conditions with which he was undertaking to cope. As a matter of fact, the party upon whose support he relied for the purpose of developing the natural resources of Mexico, and of bringing that country into line with European intellectual and industrial progress, was pledged by all its traditions to moral and political retrogression.

The enterprise, undertaken under these conditions, bore in itself such elements of failure that nothing save the force of arms and a vast expenditure of life and money could, even for a time, make it a success. Unless the French assumed direct and absolute control of Mexican affairs irrespective of party—and this contingency was specifically set aside by the most solemn declarations—they must sooner or later come into direct antagonism with allies who were pledged to the most benighted form of clericalism, and into real, though perhaps unconscious, sympathy with their opponents who stood arrayed upon the side of progress.

It was not long before the pretensions of the church and party complications caused a breach between the Corps Expeditionnaire and its original supporters, which placed the French in the unlooked-for, and by them much deprecated, attitude of invaders and conquerors of the land, equally hated by ally and foe. And yet at the outset one aspect of the situation was favorable to the success of the French undertaking.

The sweeping reforms carried out by Juarez during his brief undisturbed occupation of the country had greatly smoothed the way for the French in their self-imposed task of Mexican regeneration. The new laws had already been enforced regulating the relations of church and state. The confiscation of clergy property, the breaking up of the powerful religious orders, and religious tolerance, all had been proclaimed, as well as the freedom of the press.

Spanish, influence, which in these struggles had been exercised strongly against reform, had been abruptly brought to an end by the summary dismissal of Senor Pacheco, the Spanish minister, and the Archbishop of Mexico had been exiled.

III. M. DE SALIGNY AND M. JECKER

One of the first problems, and quite the most important, to be faced by President Juarez, upon his establishment in the capital, had been the raising of funds with which to carry on the expense of the Liberal government. As a measure the throwing upon the market of the nationalized church property recommended itself. There was, however, but little confidence, and still less ready money, in the country after many years of civil strife. So much real estate suddenly thrown upon the market depreciated property. The easy terms of sale—a third cash, the balance to be paid in pagares—tempted speculators and gave rise to many fraudulent transactions, and the measure brought little relief to the government.

Although in March, 1861, President Juarez had signed a convention adjusting anew the pecuniary claims of the French residents, on July 17 Congress found itself compelled to suspend payment on all agreements hitherto entered into with foreign powers. The very next day the representatives of France and Great Britain entered a formal protest on behalf of their governments. On

July 25, having obtained no satisfaction, they suspended all diplomatic relations with the Mexican government.

Feeling ran high between Mexicans and foreigners. The speculators in Mexican bonds, as well as more innocent sufferers, were loud in their denunciations. The Swiss banker Jecker,* who had cleverly managed to enlist the interest of powerful supporters at the court of Napoleon III, and who had become naturalized in order to add weight to his claim to French support, spared no pains in exciting the resentment of the French with regard to this violation of its pledges by the Mexican government.**

* The French claims against the Mexican government amounted to 50,000,000 francs. Jecker's interests suffered most by the decree of President Juarez of July 17,1861. Under Miramon he had negotiated, on behalf of the clerical party, the new issue of six-per-cent. bonds of 75,000,000 francs, destined to take up the old discredited government bonds, twenty-five per cent. being paid in silver by the holders, and the interest being guaranteed partly by the state, and partly by the house of Jecker. The latter was to receive a commission of five per cent. upon the transaction—3,750,000 francs. The profit to the government should have been 15,000,000 francs, had not a clause been inserted enabling Jecker to deduct his commission in advance, as well as half of the interest for five years,—11,250,000 francs,—which, as we have seen, was guaranteed by the state; so that, as a matter of fact, the government received only 3,570,000 francs. When, in May, 1860, and without the slightest warning, the house of Jecker failed, the interests of a large number of Frenchmen whose funds were intrusted to it were jeopardized; and as their only hope rested upon the profit to be derived from the issue of the bonds referred to, the decree of January 1, 1861, annulling the contract under which they had been issued, not only ruined the house of Jecker beyond recovery, but deprived its creditors of all remaining hope. Jecker then went to France. There he skilfully managed to win over to his cause some personages influential at the court of France. The Duc de Morny, whose speculative spirit was easily seduced by the golden visions of large financial enterprises in a land the wealth of which was alluringly held up to his cupidity, took him under his powerful protection. There is little doubt that this was an important factor in the Mexican imbroglio. It is interesting to know that a just Nemesis overtook Jecker, whose unworthy intrigues had brought about such incalculable mischief. He was shot by order of the Commune in 1871. See Prince Bibesco, "Au Mexique: Combats et Retraite des Six Mille" (Paris, 1887), p. 42.

** See "Revue des Deux Mondes," January, 1862, p. 766: "L'intervention des puissances avait pour avoue d'exiger une protection plus efficace pour les personnes et les proprietes de leurs sujets ainsi que l'execution des obligations contractees envers elles par la republique du Mexique."

Had France been sincere, the expedition might have seized a Mexican port as a security for the payment of such obligations, instead of spending ten times the amount of its claims in attempting to interfere with the political affairs of the country under the flimsy pretext of seeking to enforce payment thereof.

M. de Gabriac had been replaced by M. de Saligny, a creature of the Duc de Morny, whose personal interest in the Jecker bonds was freely discussed. The new minister arrived in June, 1861. His orders were to enforce recognition of the validity of the Jecker bonds. Juarez and his minister, Senor Lerdo de Tejada, peremptorily declined to "acknowledge a contract entered upon with an illegal government." There was no redress, if redress there must be, save in assuming a belligerent attitude. M. de Saligny avowedly did his utmost to aggravate the situation. Later, during the brief period of 1863-64, when the intervention seemed to hold out false promises of success, he boasted to a friend of mine that his great merit "was to have understood the wishes of the Emperor, and to have precipitated events so as to make the intervention a necessity."

This he accomplished, thanks to an incident insignificant in itself, but which he duly magnified into an unbearable insult to the French nation. On the night of August 14, 1861, a torch-light procession to celebrate the news of a victory of the government troops under General Ortega over Marquez halted before the French legation, and some voices shouted: "Down with the French! Down with the French minister!" M. de Saligny added that a shot had been fired at him from one of the neighboring azoteas, and he produced a flattened bullet in evidence. Although an investigation was immediately instituted, the result of which was to show the lack of substance of the minister's charges, the French government, then anxiously hoping for such an opportunity, supported its agent. The incident was magnified by the French papers into an "attaque a main armee contre Saligny," and at the instigation of France a triple alliance was concluded with England and Spain. On October 31, 1861, a convention was signed in London, whereby the contracting parties pledged themselves to enforce the execution of former treaties with Mexico, and to protect the interests of their citizens.* To this, as a pure matter of form, the United States was invited to subscribe. Our government, of course, declined the invitation to take advantage of the disturbed condition of the Mexican republic to enforce its claim. Mr. Seward was not then in a position to show more fully his disapproval of the action of the allied powers.

* For the correspondence upon the whole subject and the terms of the London convention, see Abbe Domenech's "Histoire du Mexique," vol. ii, p. 375 et seq.

It soon became evident that, in entering upon this treaty, the three allies had not the same end in view. As early as May 31, 1862, the French papers blamed the government for its lack of foresight in entering into a cooperation with powers whose ultimate objects so widely differed from its own.*

* See "Revue des Deux Mondes," 1862, vol. iii, p. 743.

This mistake became apparent when, on January 9, 1862, the French, under Admiral Jurien de la Graviere, and the English, under Admiral Milnes, arrived at Vera Cruz and found the Spanish division, under General Prim and Admiral Tubalco, already landed.* The conduct of their joint mission must now be determined. Already diplomacy had been brought into play by Napoleon III to induce his allies to acquiesce in his views and to consider the elevation of Maximilian to the throne of Mexico. Spain had willingly listened to the idea of establishing a monarchy, but on the condition that the monarch should belong or be closely allied to the house of Bourbon; and it stood firm upon this condition.

* The haste of Spain was regarded as an attempt to take a selfish advantage of the situation, and gave rise to some correspondence. See Domenech, loc. cit., pp. 384, 392.

IV. THE ALLIES IN MEXICO

The sound common sense of John Bull, his clearer appreciation of foreign possibilities, or perhaps the superior intelligence and honesty of his agent in Mexico, shine out brilliantly in a letter of Lord John Russell, written to the representative of England at the court of Vienna, previous to the armed demonstration made by the triple alliance.* The letter was in truth prophetic, and showed a statesmanlike grasp of the situation. He pointed out that the project of placing the Archduke Maximilian upon the throne of Mexico had been conceived by Mexican refugees in Paris; that such people were notorious for overrating the strength of their partizans in their native land, and for the extravagance of their hopes of success; that her Majesty's government would grant no support to such a project; that a long time would be necessary to consolidate a throne in Mexico, as well as to make the sovereign independent of foreign support; and that, should this foreign support be withdrawn, the sovereign might easily be expelled by the Mexican republicans. The Spanish general Prim, when later, upon the spot, he was able to appreciate the difficulties of the situation and had decided to withdraw, wrote to the Emperor a strong letter in which his views to the same effect were powerfully expressed.**

* See "La Verite sur l'Expedition du Mexique, d'apres les Documents Inedits de Ernest Louet, Payeur-en-Chef du Corps Expeditionnaire,"

edited by Paul Gaulot. Part I, "Reve d'Empire" p. 37, 4th ed. (Paris, Ollendorff, 1890).

** Ibid, p. 47.

This letter was dated "Orizaba, March 17, 1862." It is sufficiently remarkable to be given here:

"Sire: Your Imperial Majesty has deigned to write me an autograph letter which, because of the kindly expressions it contains, will become a title of honor for my posterity. . . .

"On the ground of just claims there can be no differences between the commissioners of the allied powers, and still less between the chiefs of your Majesty's forces and those of his Catholic Majesty. But the arrival at Vera Cruz of General Almonte, of the former minister Haro, of Father Miranda, and of other Mexican exiles who set forward the idea of a monarchy in favor of Prince Maximilian of Austria,—a project which, according to them, is to be backed and supported by the forces of your Imperial Majesty,— tends to create a difficult situation for all concerned, especially for the general-in-chief of the Spanish army, who, under instructions from his government based upon the convention of London, and almost the same as those given by your Majesty's government to your worthy and noble Vice-Admiral La Graviere, would find himself in the painful position of being unable to contribute to the realization of the views of your Imperial Majesty, should these look to raising a throne in this country for the purpose of placing upon it an Austrian archduke.

"Moreover, it is, sire, my profound conviction that in this country monarchical ideas find few supporters. This is logical, as this land has never known the monarchy in the persons of the Spanish sovereigns, but only in those of viceroys who governed each according to his bad or good judgment and his own lights, and all following the customs and manner of governing proper to a period which is already remote.

"Then, also, monarchy has not left here the immense interests of an ancient nobility, as was the case in Europe when, under the impulse of revolutionary storms, thrones at times were pulled down. Neither has it left high moral interests behind it, nor, indeed, anything that might induce the present generation to wish for the reestablishment of a regime which it has not known and which no one has taught it to long for or revere.

"The neighborhood of the United States, and the severe strictures of those republicans against monarchical institutions, have greatly contributed to create here a positive hatred against these. Despite disorder and constant agitation, the establishment of the republic, which took place more than forty years ago, has created habits, customs, and even a certain republican expression of thought which it cannot be easy to destroy.

"For these and other reasons which cannot escape your Imperial Majesty's high penetration, you will understand that the immense preponderance of opinion in this country is not and cannot be monarchical. If logic were not sufficient to demonstrate this, it would receive proof from the fact that, in the two months since the allied flags wave over Vera Cruz, and now that we occupy the important points of Cordoba, Orizaba, and Tohuacan, in which no other Mexican authority remains save that of the municipality, neither the conservatives nor the partizans of monarchy have made the slightest demonstration which might lead the allies to "believe" that such partisans exist.

"Be it far from me, sire, to even suppose that the might of your Imperial Majesty is not sufficient to raise in Mexico a throne for the house of Austria, Your Majesty directs the destinies of a great nation, rich in brave and intelligent men, rich in resources, and ready to manifest its enthusiasm whenever called upon to carry out your Imperial Majesty's views. It will be easy for your Majesty to conduct Prince Maximilian to the capital and to have him crowned a king; but that king will meet in the country with no other support than that of the conservative leaders, who never thought of establishing a monarchy when they were in power, and only think of it now that they are defeated, dispersed, and in exile. A few rich men will also admit a foreign monarch, if supported by your Majesty's soldiers; but that monarch will find no one to support him should your help fail him, and he would fall from the throne raised by your Majesty, as other powerful men must fall on the day when your Majesty's imperial cloak will cease to cover and protect them. I know that your Imperial Majesty, guided by your high sentiment of justice, will not force upon this nation so radical a change in its institutions if the nation does not demand it. But the leaders of the conservative party just landed at Vera Cruz say that it will be sufficient to consult the upper classes, and this excites apprehensions and inspires a dread lest violence may be done to the national will.

"The English contingent, which was to come to Orizaba, and had already prepared its means of transportation, reembarked as soon as it was known that a number of French troops larger than that stipulated in the treaty were coming. Your Majesty will appreciate the importance of their retreat.

"I beg your Imperial Majesty one thousand times pardon for having dared to submit to your attention so long a letter. But I thought that the truest way worthily to respond to the kindness of your Majesty toward me was to tell the truth, and all the truth, as I see it, upon the political conditions here. In so doing I feel that I not only fulfil a duty, but that I obey the great, noble, and respectful attachment which I feel for the person of your Imperial Majesty.

"Comte de Reus,
"General Prim."

Such warnings, however, were lost amid the glittering possibilities of so glorious an achievement. Napoleon, following his own thought, had already approached the Austrian archduke and his imperial brother with regard to the former's candidacy, and had trusted to chance as to the complications that might arise with his allies. It was not long before these became clearly defined.

The first meeting of the allies had taken place on January 10 at La Tejeria, a short distance from Vera Cruz. A proclamation to the Mexican people was issued at the instigation of General Prim. In this extraordinary document the representatives of the three great powers who had sent a combined fleet and army to obtain satisfaction for outrages committed against their flags and the life and property of their subjects, claimed to have come as friends to the support of the Mexican government.*

* See the official correspondence published by Domenech, loc. cit., vol. iii, p. 8, etc.

On the 14th the fourth conference was held. The plenipotentiaries drew up a collective note in the same tone as that of the proclamation. This was taken to the Mexican government by three commissioners. The answer to this communication was a demand for the withdrawal of the expedition. These steps had not been taken without arousing serious differences of opinion among the representatives of the powers. Moreover, the financial claims advanced by each were of such magnitude that their joint enforcement was impossible.

M. de Saligny, faithful to his premeditated plan of forcing and precipitating the catastrophe, had drawn up an ultimatum to be presented to the Mexican government, so preposterous in its pretensions that the allies could not countenance it. It could no longer be doubted that the French and the Spaniards were each playing their own game. Only the great tact and dignity of the French Commander-in-chief, Admiral Jurien de la Graviere, then prevented an open rupture.*

* Louet, loc. cit., vol. i, p. 41.

The situation had already become strained. It was soon obvious that General Prim—whether, as was alleged by the French, from personal motives,* or from a clearer insight into the true condition of the country—would side with Sir Charles Wyke, the English representative, and would help him to overrule the French leaders in their aggressive policy. He requested a conference with Senor Doblado, minister of foreign affairs, who with great shrewdness accepted the invitation. By prolonging the negotiations, the Mexican government gave a chance to the unfavorable conditions under which the expedition labored to do their very worst. Every day lost was a gain to the Mexicans. The rainy season was approaching, sickness was already decimating this army of unacclimated foreigners, and the lack of harmony between the allies was fast reaching the point of dissension. This situation was seriously aggravated by the landing in Vera Cruz (January 27) of a number of the most conspicuous among the exiles of the clerical party—General Miramon, Father Miranda, etc. These, regardless of the serious complications which their premature arrival must create for their supporters, placed themselves directly under the protection of the French.

* General Prim's wife was a rich Mexican, niece of Juarez's minister of finance, and the French minister saw in this circumstance cause to doubt the general's motives. He even accused him publicly of coveting for himself the throne of Mexico. However this may be, it seems to be a fact that when in Havana, on his way to Vera Cruz, General Prim, upon being approached by the clerical leaders, had declined in no compromising tones to recognize them, and had shown himself inclined to deal with the Liberals openly. See correspondence published by Domenech, loc. cit., vol. ii, p. 407, etc.

The force of circumstances in compelling the French to enter into negotiations with a government which they refused to recognize had already placed them in a more than awkward position. By this new complication they found themselves in the ambiguous attitude of treating with this government while shielding with their flag the outlawed representatives of a defeated rival party who had fought it as illegitimate. Not only did this exasperate the Liberals and arouse the bitterest antagonism in the country, but it gave rise to serious difficulties between the French and the English. Among the returned exiles was General Miramon, who, disregarding the inviolability of the British legation, had, while president, unlawfully taken possession of certain moneys belonging to the British government.* Sir Charles Wyke immediately requested his arrest. An angry discussion followed, the outcome of which was that Miramon, instead of being arrested on land under the shadow of the French flag, was prevented from landing and sent back to Havana.**

* This outrage was one of the main reasons for England's active cooperation in the attack upon Mexico. As far as I can ascertain the facts, $600,000 had been sent to the British legation to pay the interest upon the English bonds. At this time the foreign agents in Mexico were accused of taking advantage of their privilege to handle gold and silver without paying the circulation duty of two per cent. and the export duty of six per cent., thus illegally realizing a

considerable profit. The Mexican government was much incensed thereby, and an ugly feeling was aroused. President to Miramon, in need of funds, declared that the amount then deposited at the British legation was a commercial value liable to duties imposed by law. After some controversy upon the subject he ordered General Marquez to call upon the British government and to demand the surrender of the $600,000, to be used in the defense of the capital, at the same time declaring his willingness to recognize the debt. The minister refused. General Marquez seized the treasure, and had it taken to the palace by his soldiers. The British envoy there upon lowered his flag and retired Jalapa.

** Bibesco, loc. cit., p. 64.

On February 19 the preliminary treaty of La Soledad was signed by the allies and by Senor Doblado for the Mexican government, and on February 23 it was ratified by President Juarez. By its terms the allies were allowed, pending the negotiations having for object the adjustment of their claims, to take up their quarters beyond the limits of the unhealthful district, and to occupy the road of Mexico as far as Tehuacan and Orizaba. On the other hand, "the allies pledged themselves, should the negotiations not result in a final understanding, to vacate the territory occupied by them, and to return on the road to Vera Cruz to a point beyond the Chiquihuite, near Paso Ancho,"* i.e., in the pestilential coast region.

* Ibid., p. 49.

President Juarez only agreed to the terms, it is stated, upon the formal declaration on the part of the commissioners that "the allies had no intention to threaten the independence, the sovereignty, and the integrity of the territory of the Mexican republic."

The French contingent originally sent by Napoleon III numbered, all told, only three thousand men. As soon as the Emperor was notified of the doubtful attitude of General Prim, reinforcements numbering some forty-five hundred men had been ordered, and on March 6, 1862, General Count de Lorencez arrived at Vera Cruz to take command of the Corps Expeditionnaire.*

* Ibid., p. 36. The Spanish corps, under General Prim, numbered seven thousand. England, besides a contingent of one hundred men, furnished a fleet under Commodore Dunlap, which was to support the joint expedition.

This ended all prospect of concerted action on the part of the combined forces. The landing of these troops, which brought the French contingent to a figure far exceeding that originally agreed upon, gave umbrage to the allies* and proved, beyond the possibility of a doubt, that, notwithstanding the most explicit assurances given by the French minister of foreign affairs to the

British ambassador in Paris,** it was the intention of the French government to carry out its policy at all hazards. Moreover, the new military commander did not possess the tact and wisdom of the French admiral, whose policy had not been approved in Prance, where his signing of the convention of La Soledad had been received with dismay and disapproval.

* Compare General Prim's letter to Napoleon III, foot-note to pp. 25-27.

** "No government shall be imposed upon the Mexican people" (despatch of Lord Cowley to Lord Russell, May 2, 1862). See "L'Empereur Maximilien," etc., par le Comte Emile de Keratry, p. 11 (Leipsic, 1867). Another time the minister, M. de Thouvenel, assured Lord Cowley that negotiations had been opened by the Mexicans alone, who had gone to Vienna for the purpose (ibid.).

General de Lorencez came as the representative of the most aggressive policy, with orders to march without delay upon the capital; and there is no doubt that a worse man could not have been chosen to take the leading part in an enterprise where cool judgment was the most important requisite. Hotheaded, brave to rashness, and, if one may judge by his acts, wholly incapable of discrimination in his appreciation of the problems involved, General de Lorencez, when he arrived on the field of action, allowed himself to be misled by M. de Saligny's misrepresentations of fact. Only a bitter experience showed him his error—too late. Meantime he added to the difficulties in the way of the admiral by feeding the illusions of the French government with sanguine despatches in which he spoke in glowing terms of the "march of the French upon the capital," and of the "acclamation of Maximilian as sovereign of Mexico."

The lack of knowledge of existing conditions that characterized the French leaders in the conduct of this wretched affair was conspicuous from the very beginning of the expedition. Prince Georges Bibesco, an accomplished young Wallachian nobleman whom I knew well, and who was then on the staff of General de Lorencez's brigade, has, in his spirited account of these early events,* furnished ample evidence of the manner in which the general and his chief of staff, Colonel Valaze, were deceived as to the strength of the Liberal party by the French minister, and how they were induced by him to misrepresent the caution and judgment which the French admiral alone seems to have in some measure possessed, as an evidence of weakness and of procrastination.

* "Au Mexique, 1862: Combats et Retraite des Six Mille, par le Prince Georges Bibesco. Ouvrage couronne par l'Academie Francaise" (Paris, G. Plon, Nourrit et Cie.). Prince Bibesco was intrusted with drawing up the monthly official reports sent by the Corps Expeditionnaire to the War Office in 1862, and is therefore a trustworthy guide for that period.

In a letter addressed to the French minister of war, Marshal Randon, dated March 30, Colonel Valaze asserts his conviction that "an armed force, however small it may be, could take possession of the capital without any other difficulty than might be encountered by the commissariat to supply the army on its way." The admiral had written with a truer appreciation of the situation, and for his pains had lost the confidence of his sovereign.

V. RUPTURE BETWEEN THE ALLIES

The situation was fast reaching a crisis. An explosion was imminent. The arrival of General Almonte,* who was destined by Napoleon to be the chief executive during the regency, only hastened the rupture between the allies and precipitated the final declaration of hostilities between France and Mexico.

* March 1, 1862.

The irritation of the Mexican government knew no bounds. A decree condemning to death all traitors and reactionaries had been passed, and on March 23 it was officially communicated to the allies. On March 26 General de Lorencez joined the admiral at Tehuacan, and the latter pushed on to Orizaba, where the allies were to hold a final conference on April 9. Here General Prim and Sir Charles Wyke insisted upon the departure of the exiles, urging that their presence placed the intervention of the powers in an absolutely false light before the world.

Their secret relation to the exiles imposed upon the French the responsibility of their safety; the admiral flatly refused, at the same time announcing his intention to carry out at once the provisions of the convention of La Soledad, and to retreat with his contingent toward the coast, thereby recovering his freedom of action and the right to march upon Mexico without further delay.

It was obvious that the Mexican government was only gaining time in order to give the climate a chance to do its work. General de Lorencez, disapproving of the preliminary treaty which circumstances had forced the admiral to sign, was strongly inclined to break through its provisions and push on to the capital. He was overruled by the admiral's high sense of honor.

Measures were immediately taken to execute the articles of the convention by bringing back the French forces beyond the Chiquihuite, and on April 7 General Almonte, officially recognized by the French, endeavored to rally the scattered remnants of the clerical party by issuing a proclamation signed by ninety-two Mexican notables, in which he declared himself provisionally the supreme chief of the nation. To this President Juarez responded by a decree establishing martial law and declaring all cities occupied by the French in a state of siege. War with Mexico was declared.*

* "Where was the solemn assurance that there existed no intention to threaten the independence, the sovereignty, and the integrity of the territory of the Mexican republic? And yet, even after the repulse of the French at Puebla, Napoleon, in a letter to General Forey, dated July 3, 1862, still kept up the flimsy farce. "The end to be attained," he wrote, "is not to force upon the Mexicans a form of government which would be disagreeable to them, but to aid them in their efforts to establish, according to their own wish, a government which may have some chance of stability and "which can insure to France redress for the wrongs of which she complains" (Memorial Diplomatique, March 12, 1865). Was this blindness or duplicity?

The rupture between the allies was final, though peaceable. On April 15 Sir Charles Wyke and General Prim* concluded a separate treaty with the government of Juarez, and, having thus skilfully extricated themselves from a perilous situation, they prepared to leave the French to their own destiny.

* The instructions given to General Prim by the Spanish government were as follows: (1) A public and solemnly given satisfaction for the violent expulsion of her Majesty the Queen's ambassador (the terms of which were prescribed minutely), in the absence of which hostilities must be declared. (2) The rigorous execution of the Mon-Almonte treaty, and the payment of the Spanish claims unduly suspended by the Mexican government, and the payment in specie of 10,000,000 reals, this being the amount of unpaid interest. (3) An indemnity to the Spaniards entitled to damages in connection with the crimes committed at San Vicente, Chiconcuagua, and at the mine of San Dimas, and the punishment of the culprits and of the authorities who had failed, to punish said crimes. (4) The payment of the cost of the three-masted schooner Concepcion, captured by a ship of Juarez.

The instructions close with the following: "Such are the conditions to be presented by your Excellency, but never peace; and without their complete acceptance by the government of the republic, it will not be possible to suspend hostilities." Compare French text given by Domenech, loc. cit., p. 383.

Meantime the rainy season was approaching, at which time the difficulties, already so great, must become multiplied in a land where roads were only so called by courtesy and were little more than beaten-down tracks. The return of the French army to the coast, where the vomito was now raging, meant death to many, and possible disaster to the army. But the terms of the treaty were formal, and the admiral was not one to break his word. M. de Saligny and General de Lorencez were less punctilious; they reluctantly obeyed the order of the commander-in-chief, but watched for an opportunity to break through the impalpable barrier raised—as they thought, by honor alone—between them and the Mexican capital.

The opportunity soon presented itself, and General Zaragoza, commander-in-chief of the Liberal army, unwarily furnished General de Lorencez with the excuse for which he so anxiously longed, by addressing to him a communication concerning four hundred soldiers disabled by sickness, who had been left behind in the hospital at Orizaba under the protection of the treaty of La Soledad. In the wording of this communication the French general saw, or chose to see, a threat to the life of his soldiers.

It is but fair to say, however, that the sanguinary decrees issued one after the other by the Mexican government, the feeling against foreigners now rapidly growing among the people, the close proximity of numerous guerrillas standing ready to take advantage of the first moment of weakness or distress, the murder of French soldiers whenever they strayed from the camp,—all these symptoms of a fast fermenting spirit in the invaded land seemed to warrant the apprehensions of the general with regard to the safety of his trust.

At all events, he boldly assumed the whole responsibility of the step he was taking. Leaving Cordoba with the army, he immediately pushed on to Orizaba (April 19), where he arrived (April 20) just as General Prim, with the Spanish contingent (and the newspaper staff which, gossip related, had traveled in his suite to herald his exploits—truly a sinecure!), were leaving by the same garita on their way to the coast. General Zaragoza, with the Liberal army, retreated from the city by one gate as the French entered by the other, with all the bells of the city ringing in token of popular rejoicing—under compulsion. General Zaragoza fell back upon Puebla. Having secured Orizaba as a basis of operation, General de Lorencez, with some five thousand men, started in pursuit of the Mexican army (April 27).

In the meantime a courier from France had brought the recall of Admiral Jurien de la Graviere, whose fall from the favor of his imperial master was kept no secret. The same courier that brought the admiral the disapproval of his government brought General de Lorencez his promotion to the command of the army. Napoleon, deceived by his minister's statements, now corroborated by General de Lorencez, only later did tardy justice to the admiral, to whom he strove to make amends by attaching him to his imperial staff.

Thus the clearing up of a situation already precarious was left to a man of narrow views and small capacity, who, according to the verdict of his own officers, had little to recommend him save the soldierly qualities of bravery and energy. That General de Lorencez, under instructions from his government and relying upon the statements of its agent at Mexico, should have arrived imbued with erroneous ideas with regard to the popularity of the intervention and the relative strength of the Liberal and clerical parties, seems natural. But enough had taken place since his arrival in Mexico to open the eyes of one less wilfully blind. Any military chief of average capacity must have seen that the whole Mexican population was not rising to "greet the French army as liberators," and that the popular enthusiasm that was to open to them the doors of every town, turning their progress to the capital into a triumphal march marked at every point by ovations, showers of flowers, and the spontaneous vivas of a hitherto oppressed and now grateful multitude, was but a fast disappearing mirage luring them on to destruction.

Instead of the promised enthusiastic welcome a sullen acquiescence in the inevitable everywhere greeted the foreign invaders. This, whenever compatible with personal safety, turned into active enmity on the part of the nation, and often into open and revengeful cruelty. Instead of the great reactionary army, numbering at least ten thousand men, which, rallying under General Marquez, was to hurry to his support on his march upon the capital, a few stray guerrillas had joined his forces, ill-armed, ill-fed, undisciplined bands, upon which small reliance could be placed, and whose presence under the French flag only helped to irritate the feelings of the people. And far from the Liberal party losing its partizans upon the landing of the French, some of the reactionary leaders,—as, for instance, General Zuloaga,—forgetting their former feuds at the first sound of a foreign invasion of their native land, had rallied around the Mexican government, whose cause now seemed linked with that of the national honor.

When reverses and difficulties of all kinds assailed the army, it was remembered that General de Lorencez's violation of the sacredness of a treaty had taken place on Good Friday at half-past three o'clock, and I was told that this coincidence had been looked upon by many among the soldiers as a bad omen.

The Mexican government, however, had made good use of the time gained by the skilful negotiations of its representatives; it had earnestly prepared for resistance, and now concentrated its whole strength upon the defense of Puebla.

Such was the condition of affairs when unforeseen circumstances brought me to Mexico.

PART II.

THE FRENCH INTERVENTION

1862-1864

I. THE AUTHOR LEAVES PARIS FOR MEXICO

On March 4, 1862, one of my brothers, then on his way to the United States, and incidentally the bearer of despatches from Mr. Thomas Corwin, our minister to Mexico, was attacked and, after a sharp fight, murdered by a small band of highwaymen near Perote. I was then in Paris, where I had been left to finish my education under the care of old and dear friends. In consequence of this tragedy it was deemed advisable that I should join my family.

M. Achille Jubinal, my temporary guardian, was a distinguished antiquary and scholar, the founder of a museum in his native town, and the author of works upon ancient arms and tapestries, which are still authorities. He was an homme de lettres connected with a leading paper, and a deputy in the Corps Legislatif for the department of the Hautes-Pyrenees. He was a self-made man, and thoroughly well made was he—witty, kind, just, and learned in certain lines; and his warm Southern blood colored his personality with a shade of materialism which his refined tastes never allowed to sink to the level of coarseness.

He was to me the kindest of guardians and dearest of "chums," and made my Sundays and vacations real holidays. He often took me bric-a-brac-hunting to old shops unknown to all save the Parisian curiosity-seeker, and happy hours were spent on the quays among the old book-stands in that fascinating occupation for which the French bookworm has coined the word bouquiner. And then the charming evenings spent at the theaters and ended at Tortoni's with this truest of "boulevardiers," who knew every one and everything, and whose inexhaustible fund of anecdote was enlivened by a spontaneous easy wit and verve that made his companionship a delight.*

* Among my old papers I find the following invitation to go with him to the Odeon to see a piece called "Les Pilules du Diable":
"Je viens rappeler a Sara
Une date encore lointaine,
Et lui dire que ce sera
Le jeudi de l'autre semaine
Que la-bas a l'Odeon,
Derriere les funambules,
Sans etre M. Purgon,
Je lui fais prendre 'Les Pilules.'
"A. J."

His wife was the daughter of the Comte Rousselin de St. Albin, a man of considerable influence during the reign of King Louis-Philippe, whose close personal friend he was.

M. de St. Albin's house in the Rue Vieille du Temple, where his family lived when we first knew them, had originally formed part of the famous Temple, which in medieval times was the abode of the Templars. It was an interesting place, full of historic memories. Within these legendary walls he had accumulated countless relics of those among his early associates who were then so fast becoming heroes in the French annals. Being an intimate friend and a connection of the Comte de Barras, the chief executive under the Directory, it was to him that the latter, by will dated February 2, 1827, intrusted not only his secret memoirs,* but all his private and official papers. At the death of M. de St. Albin (1847) this important collection passed to the possession of his children.

*See "Memoires de Barras," vol. i, p. 20 (Paris, 1895-96). These memoirs have only recently been published by M. Georges Duruy, who married M. Jubinal's daughter, the granddaughter of Comte Rousselin de St. Albin.

I well remember, as a little girl, being shown some of the choicest pieces in the series, among which were interesting original portraits. One paper especially made an indelible impression upon my childish mind, and I can now recall the feeling of awe with which I gazed upon the appeal to arms in the name of the Commune, drawn up by Robespierre and his colleagues on the night of the 9th Thermidor, a document which has since been published by M. Duruy in the "Memoires de Barras." Robespierre had just written the first syllable of his name below those of his colleagues when the Convention was attacked. The blood-stains which spattered the sheet, and told of the final tragedy of the leader's life, appealed to my youthful imagination, and are still vivid in my memory.

Notwithstanding her father's connections with the Orleanists, Hortense de St. Albin and her brother were closely connected with the new order of things. She had entertained personal relations with the Empress before her elevation to the imperial throne, and the brother, Comte Louis-Philippe de St. Albin, was librarian to her Majesty. These close affiliations with the court did not prevent M. Jubinal, in his political capacity, from gradually sliding into the ranks of the opposition. Later he occasionally was one of the few who voted against the measures of the government in the legislative struggles brought about by the intervention of France in Mexican affairs. Whether this attitude was wholly due to his superior common sense, or whether behind his political convictions there lingered a tinge of chagrin at a disappointed hope of senatorial honors once held out to his ambition by the French emperor, it is difficult to tell. It is probable that the latter motive formed, unknown to him, a foundation upon which his wisdom and political principles rested, and which lent them added solidity.

Before I left France I was, at his house, the interested though silent listener to many a violent discussion upon the stirring theme. The critics of the Napoleonic policy loudly denounced the fraudulent transactions connected with the issue of the Jecker bonds. They more than intimated that the great of the land were mixed up in the disgraceful agiotage that had led to these serious difficulties, and that all this brilliant dust of a civilizing expedition to a distant El Dorado was raised about the Emperor by his entourage to conceal from him what was going on nearer home.

One of their strongest arguments was that the invasion of Mexico by the French army must necessarily give umbrage to the United States, with which traditions of friendship had long existed; and they urged that, whatever the crippled condition of the Union, such a course could not fail eventually to lead to dangerous complications.

One day in March, 1862, before the news of the rupture between the French and their allies had reached Paris, M. Jubinal invited me to accompany him to the Hotel des Ventes, Rue Drouot, where an important collection of tapestries and other objects of art was on view to be sold. There were comparatively few amateurs in the rooms when we entered. My companion was pointing out to me the beauties of a piece which he particularly coveted when some one came behind us and called him by name. We both turned around and faced a middle-aged man whose dress, manner, and general bearing showed him to be a personage of some importance. M. Jubinal, who evidently knew him well, addressed him as "M. le Duc," and his strong likeness to the Emperor, as well as a few stray words, soon led me to guess, even before my guardian had gone through the form of an introduction, that he was no less a personage than the Duc de Morny.

The Duc de Morny's position during the period that elapsed between the revolution of 1848 and 1865 was one unique in France; and yet it is doubtful whether his fame would have been as worldwide as it has become had it not been for the part he played in the Mexican imbroglio.

Brought up as a child by a charming woman of graceful intellect and literary pretensions, he had met early in life the Duc d'Orleans, who had led him into the gay Parisian world of which he was the leader. After a brief military career in Africa, he resigned from the army, and divided his interest between politics and speculation. He employed his leisure moments in writing very indifferent plays, which, although published under a nom de guerre (St. Remy), he depended upon the servility of the Parisian press to carry through. He was not a deep thinker, nor was his intellectual horizon a broad one; but his views were liberal, his shallow mind was brilliant and versatile, and to the graceful frivolity of a man of the world he united a taste for the serious financial and political problems of his time. He belonged to that set of bright young politicians who, toward the end of the reign of Louis-Philippe, passed, as was cleverly said, "from a jockey club to the Chamber of Deputies," declaring that France was a victim of old-fogyism, and flattering themselves with the thought that they would infuse the vigor of youth into politics. These would-be founders of a new era called themselves "progressive conservatives" (conservateurs progressistes).*

* Under this title he wrote an article published in the "Revue des Deux Mondes," January, 1, 1848.

Just before the revolution of July, which established the republic, he was spoken of for a place in the cabinet as minister of commerce. Gifted with great tact and worldly wisdom, satisfied to wield power without taking too large a place on the political stage, the Duc de Morny's popularity and peculiar position enabled him to be the go-between in the compromise that followed. As early as 1849 he was reported to have said to a friend: "Quand je coup se fera je vous en previens, c'est moi qui le ferai."* Another of his mots has often been quoted** and is most characteristic of the man: "S'il y a un coup de balai, je tacherai d'etre du cote du manche."

* "Revue des Deux Mondes," 1865, vol. lvi, p. 501 et seq.

** Henri Rochefort ("Les Aventures de ma Vie," vol. i, p. 245) casts a doubt upon the originality of his wit.

At the time when I met him he was president of the Corps Legislatif, where, without the slightest pretension to oratorical talent, he wielded an immense influence. He was what we call a "leader" in every sense of the word—at court, on the Bourse, and in the political as well as in the social world.

On that morning he was with the duchess, bent upon the same errand as ourselves, and seeing us, he had come to ask M. Jubinal to give them his opinion upon the value of a possible purchase. After discussing the subject, which was all-engrossing for the moment, the duchess turned to me and politely drew me into conversation. Her kindly manner set me at ease, and she soon extracted from me the information that I was about to sail for Mexico. At this she became much excited, and exclaiming, "Oh, I must tell M. de Morny!" she immediately moved to where he and M. Jubinal had wandered, saying, "Just think, this young girl is going to Mexico on the Louisiane alone, under the care of strangers." A gleam of interest brightened the great man's dull eye as for a moment it rested upon me. He asked me a few questions; but as the duchess rather commanded my attention, he soon turned to M. Jubinal, and I overheard my guardian telling him of the tragic events which had caused my rather sudden departure, at the same time expressing some anxiety with regard to my own safety. "Oh," said the duke, "by the time she arrives there we will have changed all that. Lorencez is there now; our army will then be in the city of Mexico; the roads will be quite safe. Have no fear."

A mild, half-playful argument followed in the course of which my guardian, I thought, was not quite as uncompromising in his criticism as he was when surrounded by those who shared his own opinions. But the duke was very affable, and the duchess was in truth charming, with her Northern beauty, her delicate high-bred features, and her wealth of blond hair. No wonder if he could not be stern.

It was the first time that I had met the man whose influence then ruled over the destinies of France and Mexico, and the incident naturally impressed itself upon my memory. Upon my arrival in Mexico, where I found men puzzling over the extraordinary lack of concert between the allied invaders, which baffled their understanding, I remembered those words of the Duc de Morny, uttered even before a suitable pretext had been furnished General de Lorencez for breaking through the preliminary treaty of La Soledad, and, of course, before the news of the final rupture between France, England, and Spain could possibly have reached Europe. M. de Lorencez, it is now known, had gone to Mexico with ORDERS to march without delay upon the capital.

The Gare d'Orleans presented a scene of more than usual animation when, on the morning of the thirteenth day of April, 1862, our fiacre landed us at its entrance, en route for St. Nazaire. The Compagnie Transatlantique, formed by the house of Pereire, was giving a grand inaugural banquet to celebrate the opening of the new line of steamers that was to carry passengers direct from France to Mexico. The Louisiane was to sail on her first trip on the following day. A special train was on the track awaiting the distinguished guests of the company, and it is safe to say that two thirds of the celebrities of the day in the world of finance, of politics, and of journalism were gathering upon the platform.

M. Jubinal, himself an invited guest, had decided to take me with him, as he was anxious to see me safely on board. The presence of a young girl at the station naturally excited some curiosity among the small clusters of men who here and there stood by the carriage doors chatting with one another, ready to take their places; and as we passed by, my companion was the object of inquiring looks from those with whom he was on familiar terms. But this curiosity invariably gave way to evidences of more earnest interest when they were told that I was to sail for Vera Cruz on the following day.

Our companions in the railway-carriage were journalists whom M. Jubinal knew, and a deputy whose name now escapes my memory. Each one had much advice to bestow and many wise opinions to express, the remembrance of which afforded me endless amusement after I had reached my destination, so far were they from meeting the requirements of the case. And all, whatever their personal views with regard to the intervention, confidently expressed the conviction that upon reaching the capital I should find the French flag flying over the citadel.

During the ride down to St. Nazaire the conversation ran wholly upon the subject of Mexico, and of the magnificent opportunities to French commerce and speculation opened up by the expedition. Of these our present errand was an earnest. In listening to them, one might have thought that Napoleon had found Aladdin's lamp, and had deposited it for permanent use at the Paris Bourse. Mining companies, colonization companies, railroad companies, telegraph companies, etc.,—all the activities that go to constitute the nineteenth-century civilization,—were in a few short years to develop the mining and agricultural resources of the country. A new outlet would open to French industry, and the glory of French arms would check the greed of the Anglo-Saxon, that arrogant merchant race who would monopolize the trade of the world. The thought was brilliant, grand, generous, noble, worthy of a Napoleonic mind. There were millions in it!

Later, upon reaching Vera Cruz, I remembered that nothing had been said of the yellow fever and the rainy season, or of the magnitude of the sparsely populated country which it was necessary to clear of predatory bands who then virtually held it, or of the expense in men and millions which must be incurred to maintain order while all these great schemes were being carried out. My eloquent fellow-travelers unhesitatingly asserted that Mexico yearned for all this prosperity; it was extending its arms to France; the French army would receive one long ovation in its triumphant march to the capital amid vivas and showers of roses. All who KNEW said so. How lucky was mademoiselle to be going there at this auspicious moment, to witness such great and stirring events!

M. Jubinal looked somewhat incredulous, but the atmosphere created just then by the occasion was certainly against him. Here was a large company of French capitalists, backed by one of the most substantial houses in France, opening direct communication between that country and Mexico, when hitherto most of the traffic had been conducted through an English medium. To my youthful mind it DID seem then as though M. Jubinal had the worst of the argument.

Upon leaving my brilliant companions to find my way to the steamer, however, the scene changed as suddenly as though a wizard's wand had wrought its magic. The weather seemed threatening; a dull gray sky hung low over the bay, and the chopping, white-capped waves reflected the leaden color of the clouds.

There were only forty passengers on board, and, comparatively speaking, little of the animation that usually precedes the outgoing of an ocean steamer. I found without difficulty the French banker and his Mexican wife who had kindly consented to chaperon me during my lonely journey; and I soon discovered that she and I were the only women passengers on board.

Our fellow-travelers were uninteresting—mostly commercial agents or small tradesmen representing the old-established petty commerce with Mexico. The new order of things was suggested, somewhat ominously, only by the presence of two young surgeons on their way to increase the effective force of the military hospital in Vera Cruz.

Evidently the predicted exodus to El Dorado had not yet begun. Where was the advance-guard of the great army of emigrant capitalists now about to start, and of which I had just heard so much?

This was the first serious disillusion of my life, and it left a deep and permanent impression upon my mind. What was the relation between the great banquet of Pereire & Co., this train full of statesmen, literati, and other distinguished men, this blast of the press heralding a great and joyful event in the commercial life of the French nation,—and this old patched-up ship, with its scant load of commonplace and evidently old Franco-Mexican tradesmen, lying in lonely dullness against the gray sky on that gloomy evening?

Those men were rejoicing over us while we lay here at anchor. They were drinking to phantoms evoked by their own imagination, and their glowing speeches would to-morrow stir the fancy of thousands of readers who, seeing through their eyes, would view the dark hulk of our old ship framed in a glittering golden cloud. Where I now stood, almost alone in the gloom, the vivid imagination of those men yonder in the banquet-hall at that very hour perceived the mirage of the speculative fever crowding the decks of the Pereire steamers with imaginary colonists eager to convert their savings into mining stocks and Mexican railroad bonds, and rushing to the land of Montezuma to sow and reap a rich harvest for Prance.

How many wretches were induced to risk their money upon such representations?* Oh, the dreariness, the loneliness, of that first night at anchor in the Bay of Biscay! The misgivings that filled my heart! Who was right? What should I find over there? Surely these statesmen, capitalists, journalists, legislators, should know what they were doing.

* "L'Opinion Nationale," August 30, 1866, stated that 300,000 bondholders invested in Mexican securities which in 1866 were worth no more than the paper they were printed on.

And yet, beyond the line of the western horizon, which only a few hours before they had peopled with glittering visions, there slowly rose in the darkness the phantom of an arrested coach, of panic-stricken travelers, of fierce murderers assaulting a young man, of a dead body on the roadside; and this empty ship seemed more real at that moment than all that I had yet heard or read.

After stopping to coal at Fort-de-France, in the beautiful island of Martinique, and a few days later stopping at Santiago de Cuba, we finally, on May 2, caught sight of a dark, broadening line upon the horizon, behind which soon loomed up in solitary dignity the snow-capped peak of Orizaba; and passing the Cangrejos and the island of Sacrificios, we anchored off the fort of San Juan de Ulloa, where we awaited a clean bill of health from the quarantine officers who came on board.

The first impression made upon the mind by Vera Cruz is depressing. In May the heat is intense. The town is situated in a low, swampy district, and was then unprovided with the slightest artificial contrivance for the betterment of its naturally unhygienic conditions. There was no systematic drainage, and the entire refuse matter of an ignorant and indolent population might have been left to fester under the rays of a tropical sun during the dry season, had it not been for the zopilotes, or turkey-buzzards, which, protected by law, had multiplied to such an extent as to form a tolerably efficient body of scavengers. The steeples and flat roofs of the low town were literally black with them. Their dense black swarms, resting like a pall upon it, in striking contrast with its white walls, gave the city, as one approached it from the sea, an appearance of mourning. On our journey we had anchored at Santiago de Cuba, where smallpox was raging, and now the health-officers hesitated about letting us enter this plague-stricken place.

As time wore on, the excitement of our safe arrival gradually died out. We gazed across the water at the inhospitable gates to this promised land, where so many strangers pausing like ourselves had recently found a grave. It seemed as though we were awaiting admittance to a funeral; and when the tolling of some church or convent bell, frightening the carrion-eating birds, caused a general flutter, the sight was strangely suggestive of the pestilential death ever lurking below, ready to feed upon the foreign visitor. One could scarcely help thinking of the dead and the dying, and wondering, with a shudder, what might not be the ignoble cravings of the gruesome flock.

II. PUEBLA AND MEXICO—GENERAL DE LORENCEZ—GENERAL ZARAGOZA

The health-officers who boarded the steamer at Vera Cruz gave us unexpected and startling news. The French army had been repulsed with serious loss before Puebla. The direct route, by which the trip from Vera Cruz to Mexico via Orizaba—one hundred and ten leagues—could be made in four days,* was blocked by the contending armies. If we wished to proceed on our journey, we must do so via Jalapa, a much longer route. The discomforts of this road were, moreover, complicated by the fact that it was now infested by a large number of guerrillas,—one might as well say highwaymen,—who made it difficult for travelers to pass unmolested, unless through some special arrangement. This my companions were confident could easily be settled; but some days might be spent in negotiations, and the health-officers said that the yellow fever was raging as it had not raged for years. The presence of so many foreigners had added to its violence, and the French garrison could be maintained only by constant reinforcements.

* It can now be made by rail in ten hours.

Upon landing, our little party went directly to the house of Mr. Lelong, the hospitable French banker who in Vera Cruz represented the house of Labadie & Co. Here we remained five days, enjoying every comfort, while the necessary preparations were being made for our somewhat perilous journey to the capital. I then heard for the first time the details of the disaster brought upon the French by General de Lorencez's wilful blindness.

Confident in the elan of his picked troops, and, as one of his officers afterward told me, complacently holding up to himself the example of Cortez, who had conquered the land with as many hundreds as he had thousands, the French general, unable with so small a force to undertake a siege, determined to attempt the assault of the Cerro de Guadalupe. This fort dominated the place, and its possession must, in his opinion, insure the fall of Puebla.

The ill-advised attack was made on May 5,1862, with twenty-five hundred men. The place was topographically strong. It was defended by General Zaragoza with the very pick of the Mexican army under General Negrete, and was, moreover, supported by the well-manned battery of the Fort de Loretto. To attempt the assault of such a position without the support of artillery seemed madness; and when the general ordered his troops forward it was found that his field-battery, owing to the lay of the land, could not even be brought to bear upon the fort at sufficiently close range to reach it. One fifth of the corps of attack was thus uselessly sacrificed.

Some months after these events (September, 1862) I witnessed in the city of Mexico the public obsequies of General Zaragoza,* whom this exploit had naturally placed high in the esteem of his countrymen. Upon the elevated catafalque, drawn by a long line of horses draped in black trappings, lay the stately coffin. Tossed at its feet was the French flag; banners, hung everywhere, inscribed with devices recalling his signal service to his country, proclaimed him "the conqueror of conquerors" (el conquistador de los conquistadores). The French, it was asserted, had measured themselves with and conquered all the nations of the world, and Zaragoza had conquered the French!

* Much of the credit for the achievement was due to General Negrete, whose command bore the weight of the assault upon the Cerro de Guadalupe and prevented its capture.

This day is proudly recorded in the Mexican annals as the Cinco de Mayo. The historic importance of a battle is not always to be measured by the numbers of the contending forces, and although its far-reaching significance was at the time scarcely understood, this check must ever be remembered by future historians as the first serious blow struck by fortune at Napoleon III and his fated empire. The honor of France was now involved and must be vindicated. There was no receding upon the dangerous path. No French sovereign could dare to withdraw without avenging the first check met with by the French army since Waterloo, and thus was the Emperor rushed on to fulfil his own destiny. To-day the fire from the fort of Guadalupe casts a flash of lurid light upon the beginning of la debacle, and upon the last chapters written at Sedan. During the whole of that fatal day the doomed men marched, as they were ordered to march, upon the Mexican battery. They hopelessly fought, and died heroically; and when night came they beat an orderly retreat, carrying away with them most of their wounded.

General de Lorencez slowly fell back upon Orizaba, where he issued a proclamation* to the army, openly laying the responsibility of the disaster upon the false statements made to him by the French representative.

* See proclamation, published in Louet, "La Verite sur l'Expedition du Mexique," etc. "Reve d'Empire," p. 72.

The French army, which fell back upon Orizaba, was in a critical position. Its communications with the coast had been interrupted by the Liberal guerrillas, and it was completely cut off from the seaport and from France. The bridges were destroyed; the convoys of provisions were attacked and burned; anxiety was felt by the commissariat with regard to supplies. The garrisons left by the French on the way had been driven back and hemmed in in the unhealthful region, where the French regiments were fairly melting away, and no courier was permitted to bring news from the seat of war to the French fleet and to the garrison of Vera Cruz.

The rainy season was near at hand when communication was restored by the arrival at Vera Cruz of General Felix Douay, who landed with reinforcements on May 16.

The five days that we spent in Vera Cruz were anxious days for those who had assumed the responsibility of our little party. Never was there a worse time to travel over a road which at best was unsafe, and yet we could not remain where we were without danger.

I was not allowed to move out of the house and all I saw of the town was from the balcony whence, in the cool of the evening, I looked down upon the dull street. Every now and then a passing stretcher supporting a covered human form would remind us that we were in a plague-stricken city, and make us eager to start upon our way.

At last arrangements were completed, terms were made with a small guerrilla band whose chief undertook to see us safely through to Mexico, and on May 27 we began our journey.

The men of our escort, whom we met just out of the city, were a ruffianly-looking set. The chief had received an ugly saber-cut across his face, which added to the forbidding expression of a naturally repulsive physiognomy. They were well mounted, however, and seemed inclined to be civil. We were allowed only an arrota (twenty-five pounds) of luggage, and were supposed to have no money with us; but on the night before we left we sewed a few ounces of gold (sixteen-dollar pieces) in unlikely places of our underwear. Thus we left Vera Cruz a la grace de Dieu.

Well it was that we had made terms with this little guerrilla company, and we had ample opportunity of testing the truth of the saying, "There is honor among thieves." All along the road we met armed bands, varying in strength, until, at a village near Jalapa, we fell in with the well-known chief Antonio Perez and his famous plateados, two hundred strong, who had won their name and a somewhat doubtful distinction by their successful raids upon convoys of silver. Our escort fraternized with all, and they let us pass unmolested.

I was told that at this period scarcely a stage reached the capital without having been robbed. The passengers were often even despoiled of their clothing, so that newspapers were brought into requisition to serve as garments for the unfortunate victims. When such was the case the doors of the hotel were closed upon the arrival of the coach in the courtyard, and blankets or other coverings were brought down before the travelers could alight with any show of propriety.

To say nothing of our emotions, many and varied were our experiences on that never-to-be-forgotten nine days' journey. Generally we slept in cities or towns, where we were made more or less comfortable; but on one occasion, owing to an accident, we were belated and had to stop overnight at a miserable hamlet, where no accommodation could be procured save such as a native adobe house could afford. This consisted of one large room approached by a shed. In this room the man, his wife, his children, his dogs, pigs, and small cattle lived. A team of mules outside put in their heads through an opening and breathed over our cots. The English language cannot be made to describe the atmosphere and other horrors of that night. Cots had been improvised for Mrs. D—— and me, but there was no sleep for us, and we envied the men, who took their chances of malaria and preferred sleeping outside to sharing our shelter.

At last we reached the crest of the mountain from which we looked down upon the valley of Mexico, a huge basin encircled by mountains; and there at our feet lay the capital, with its two hundred thousand souls, its picturesque buildings, and the lakes of Chalco and Tezcuco, while to one side the huge snow-capped volcanoes, the Iztaccihuatl and the Popocatepetl, like two gigantic sentries, seemed to watch over the sacredness of this classical spot of Mexican history.

The capital was quiet and peaceful. It seemed utterly shut out from all the excitement created by the invasion, as though, really trusting in its remoteness, its barriers of mountains, its lakes and natural defenses, it defied the foreigner. Was it that Mexico was then so accustomed to transfer its allegiance from one military ruler to the other that even foreign invasion left it indifferent? Or was it the childlike faith in the unknown, the national Quien sabe? spirit, virtually carried out at this supreme crisis? However this may have been, very little of the outside conflict seemed as yet to have penetrated the minds of the people. The diplomatic corps entertained our little coterie, which included those Mexicans who were willing to mix with the foreign element.

Society danced and flirted, rode in the Paseo, and walked in the Alameda, just as though the Cinco de Mayo had been a decisive battle and General de Lorencez's army had been driven back to its ships.

The bull-fights once in a while gathered in the vast enceinte of the Plaza de Toros the society of the capital. During the winter of 1863 the young men of fashion of Mexico took the Plaza de Toros, and invited Mexican society to a performance. All who took part were amateurs, and it was a brilliant affair. The huge amphitheater, crowded with the well-dressed audience, was in itself a memorable spectacle, and as the sun went down, casting great shadows and oblique rays of light upon the gay assemblage, intent upon the fierce games of the picturesque performers in the arena, one unconsciously dreamed of the Colosseum and of the bloody sports of semibarbarous Rome.

Besides the ordinary bull-fight, there were many exercises of horsemanship and with the lasso that did credit to the skill of the young gentlemen. Moreover, as these men, who were all wealthy, rode their own spirited horses, the performance presented none of the most revolting features of the usual bull-fight, where the poor, miserable hacks, too jaded to obey the rein, are generally gored, and soon turn the arena into a slaughter-house, the sight of which it is impossible for an Anglo-Saxon to endure.

Our box was sent us by Don Jose Rincon Gallardo and his brother Don Pedro, who belonged to the elite of Mexican society and were among the prime movers in the affair. When Mexico fell into the power of the enemy, these young men joined the Liberal army in defense of their native land, and later we will find the first at Queretaro earning honorable distinction amid events the memory of which can never fade from the pages of history.

It was a curious, easy life in the midst of what to us now would seem perilous conditions. No man, in those days, ventured out of an evening to pay a call without being well armed, and our little anteroom assumed, after eight o'clock, the appearance of an arsenal. Nor were these precautions unwarranted. To give but one instance: The secretary of the Prussian legation, a nephew of the minister, Baron Wagner, having excited certain animosities, was more than once waylaid and attacked in the street after dark. He was a fine specimen of the Teutonic race, a tall, powerful man, and generally carried brass knuckles. After the first attack he made it a point at night to walk in the middle of the street, so as to avoid too close a proximity with corners and dark angles of doorways, regarding them as possible ambushes. As he was fully prepared, he more than once escaped without harm. But one night, when, for some unknown reason, he carried a revolver, he was assaulted from behind. Before he could cock his weapon and turn to face his would-be assassins, he had received several stabs in the back, and was left as dead upon the street. He lay for weeks between life and death.

This had happened in the spring of 1862. A short time after my arrival, having just recovered, he called to take leave of my family before returning to Germany. His faith in the superiority of brass knuckles over the revolver, in case of sudden attack, was not to be shaken.

Many and strange were the stories told me when I arrived in that land destined by nature to be a paradise, but of which the inhabitants were then making a Tartarus. To the horrors then perpetrated by robbers or highwaymen, justice could be done only by the pen of a Poe.

Kidnapping was not infrequent, and the cruel ingenuity displayed by the bandits to keep safely their victim pending the negotiations for a ransom was often blood-curdling. I might fill a small volume with such anecdotes, but the terrible fate of two hacendados, kidnapped in the interior of the country, may suffice to give an idea of the tax which living in Mexico at that time might levy upon the emotions of a young girl fresh from Paris.

The two unfortunate men had been captured by one of those small bands which in war-times were called guerrillas, but which we should ordinarily call banditti. They were dragged from place to place about the country by their captors, who kept them under strict surveillance. One evening, as they were approaching a town, the prospect of a riotous night spent over pulque and monte at some fonda excited the imagination of the men, and, as no one would consent to be deprived of the anticipated pleasure for the sake of mounting guard over the prisoners, it was decided that the miserable victims should be, for safe-keeping, buried up to their necks in the earth. Surely they could not escape, and would be there next morning awaiting the return of their captors. And so they no doubt would have been, but for the coyotes, which, allured by the easy prey delivered up to them by the devilish ingenuity of those human fiends, came during the night and devoured the heads of the helpless victims. Who can ever realize the mental and physical anguish in the midst of which those two wretched lives came to an end?

Sometimes there was a touch of weird humor in the manner in which such outrages were perpetrated. One night a wealthy family in Mexico drove home in their carriage from a party. They stopped at their porte-cochere, which was opened by their servant, and closed tight behind them as they drove in. Two men, however, had fastened on to the carriage behind. They overpowered the portero as he barred the door, while the noise of the carriage rolling on the flags of the patio smothered the sound of the scuffle. They opened the door to their accomplices, and easily overcame family and servants, all of whom were bound hand and foot. Then the robbers ransacked the premises, and having packed all the valuables into the carriage, one of them took the coachman's clothes, mounted on the box, and coolly drove off in style—carriage, horses, and all.

In a wild, sparsely populated country like Mexico in 1862, where communication was difficult, where the police of even large cities, when not in direct sympathy with the malefactors, were overawed by them, and where forty years of civil war had hardened men to the sight of blood, it is not to be wondered at if impunity had multiplied such occurrences and destroyed all sensibility with regard to human suffering.

Much excitement was created both in France and in the United States, during the French intervention, by the relentless spirit with which the conflict was conducted between the opposing parties, and by the wanton destruction of life and property which characterized the struggle. But when one realizes that the Mexican armies at that time were on both sides to a great extent made up of such predatory material, and that even their officers were frequently little more than chiefs of guerrillas, who rallied sometimes under one flag, sometimes under the other, but in either case were always ready for rapine, the brutal character of the conflict can scarcely excite surprise.

III. THE SIEGE OF PUEBLA—GENERAL FOREY—GENERAL ORTEGA

The news of the check sustained by the French at Puebla—a check to which the precarious condition of the army lent all the proportions of a serious defeat—was made public in France by means of a despatch sent from New York on June 14. The army was at once raised to twenty-five thousand men. The command-in-chief of this increased force was given to General Forey. He entered upon his official duties on October 25,1862.*

* General Forey commanded the Fourth Division at the battle of Alma, in the Crimean war; at Sebastopol he commanded both the Third and the Fourth, to which was intrusted the siege work.

The new commander-in-chief, like those whom he was superseding, was under precise orders from the home government to be guided by M. de Saligny. Notwithstanding the disastrous consequences of his misrepresentations, the French minister, strangely enough, still retained his hold upon the Emperor and his advisers.

General Forey's instructions, given in a note from Napoleon dated July 3, 1862, were to bring about, through General Almonte, the convocation of an assembly of notables to decide upon the "form of government and the destinies of Mexico." Should the Mexicans prefer a monarchy, "it was in the interest of France to support them, and to indicate the Archduke Maximilian as the candidate of France."*

* "La Verite sur l'Expedition du Mexique, d'apres les Documents Inedits d'Ernest Louet," etc. Edited by Paul Gaulot. Part I, "Reve d'Empire," p. 91, 4th ed.(Paris).

On February 18, 1863, after wasting four precious months, at an enormous cost of money and prestige, General Forey appeared before Puebla.* The procrastination of the French commander had given the Mexican government time to elaborate the defense. General Zaragoza had died, in the full blaze of his glory, in the month of September. His successor, General Jesus Gonzalez Ortega, had now under his command a fairly organized army of twenty-two thousand men. The main trouble was the scarcity of arms. The guns were mostly old rejected muskets, and I was told that during the siege unarmed bodies of men waited to use the arms of the slain or wounded. But the place had been strongly fortified; this time it was to be war in earnest.

* General Forey explained his extraordinary procrastination by complaining that the minister of war had failed to supply him with a sufficient amount of ammunition. See Colonel Loizillon, "Lettres sur l'Expedition du Mexique," p. 101.

The town was built in blocks. Each block, fortified and defended by the besieged, must be fought for and carried by assault, at terrible cost of life on the part of the French, whose close ranks were fired upon with murderous effect from the roofs and windows on both sides of the streets.

The episodes of the contest recall those of the siege of Saragossa, when the Spaniards so fiercely resisted the French forces; only at Puebla the cruel struggle lasted two whole months.* To quote a French officer, it was "a noble defense, admirably organized."

* From March 18 to May 10, 1863. See Colonel Loizillon, "Lettres sur l'Expedition du Mexique," Paris, 1890.

The pulse of the capital now quickened under the influence of Puebla's sacrifice to the national honor. Every now and then a thrill of vindictive patriotism ran through the city and clamored for revenge. Already, before the celebration of the anniversary of the national independence (September 16, 1862), wild rumors of a contemplated wholesale slaughter of foreigners had run through the town, arousing among us fears of an impending catastrophe. The news had one day been brought us that the 16th was the date fixed for these new Sicilian Vespers, and all were warned to be watchful. The day, however, passed without any further demonstration of ill will than a few shots, and cries of "Mueran los Franceses!"

Much of this excitement had, of course, been fostered by the stirring proclamations of the government, issued with a proper desire to arouse into something like patriotic enthusiasm the apathy of a people accustomed to submit to the inevitable. There was no telling, however, to what extremes might resort a populace composed of Indians and half-breeds, should it once become fully alive to the situation. To such a people geographical discrimination seemed a nicety; the issue was between them and the foreigners, and the words "French" and "foreigner" were at that time generally used as synonymous.

This was not all. When the fort of San Xavier was taken, and when began the frightful hand-to-hand fight in Puebla, the result of which was a foregone conclusion, the government announced its intention to defend the capital. The level of the lakes of Chalco and Tezcuco is above that of the city, and the flooding of the valley was regarded as an effective means of defense. This, of course, meant pestilence. The president resolutely declared that, should arms fail, the people must prolong the defense of the capital with their "teeth and nails"; and although there was no practical response among the people, a general and very genuine uneasiness pervaded the whole community.

It was a Mexican custom on Good Friday to burn Judas in effigy on the Plaza Mayor. Judas was a manikin made in the shape of the person who happened to be most unpopular at the time. It was quite admissible to burn Judas under different shapes, and sometimes these summary autos da fe were multiplied to suit the occasion and the temper of the people. At the same time, rattles were sold on the streets, and universally bought alike by children and adults, by rich and poor, to grind the bones of Judas, and the objectionable noise—second in hideousness only to that of our own sending off of fire-crackers on the Fourth of July—was religiously kept up all day. In the year of our Lord 1863 Judas was burned in Mexico on the Plaza Mayor under the shapes of General Forey, Napoleon III, and last, but not least, M. Dubois de Saligny, who especially was roasted with a will amid the wild execrations of the populace.

President Juarez had bent his whole energy upon the raising of an army of relief. He succeeded in getting together some ten thousand men, the command of whom he gave to General Comonfort. This had been no easy task. A general leva had been ordered, and all were mustered into the army who could be provided with arms. Of uniforms there was, of course, no mention. It was a supreme and desperate effort.

A convoy of supplies for the relief of General Ortega was also prepared, which it was hoped General Comonfort might succeed in throwing into the besieged city. He utterly failed, however; and his raw recruits having been routed at San Lorenzo* by General Bazaine (May 8), further resistance became hopeless. Puebla was lost. General Ortega faced the situation with a dignity worthy of his courageous defense of the town. He spiked his guns, blew up his magazines, disbanded the garrison, and, with his officers, surrendered on May 19.

* San Lorenzo is a village and hacienda through which the main road to Puebla passes about sixty-six miles from Mexico.

The news fell like a knell upon the capital. As far as we were concerned, there seemed to be just then only a choice of evils. Either the government would await in Mexico the impending issue, and we must be exposed to all the unspeakable horrors of which Puebla had just been the scene, or the President and his administration would abandon the city, and an interval must follow during which we must be left exposed to mob law, or, should Marquez first take possession of the city, perhaps to pillage and bloodshed.

Meanwhile Congress had indefinitely adjourned, after conferring full and extraordinary powers upon Juarez. The president issued a proclamation announcing his firm resolve to continue the war. After this he prepared to leave the city and to retire to San Luis.

That night, while sitting in our drawing-room, we heard the dull, steady tramp of men marching, otherwise noiselessly, down the Calle de San Francisco toward the plaza; and looking out of the window, we saw the debris of the defeated Liberal army making its way through the city. A strange, weird sight they presented in the moonlight—these men whose sole equipment consisted of a musket and a cartridge-box slung over their white shirts. Most of them wore only loose calzoneras, and many, according to the Mexican custom, were accompanied by their women. Apparently undrilled, or, at least, tramping on with scarcely an attempt at order, and seen in the half-shadow cast by the houses upon the moonlit street, their loose ranks reminded one more of the immigration of some ancient barbaric horde than of the march of a modern army.

I shall never forget the impressions of that night. The picturesqueness of the scene was not lessened by the element of personal interest that attached to it. What did this portend—this ragged remnant of a defeated army hurrying through the capital in the dead of night? Were the French approaching, driving it before them? Was it intended to garrison the city, and here to make the last stand in defense of the republic and of Mexican liberty? Or, on the contrary, was it beating a retreat into the interior of the country, making way for the advent of the foreigner and monarchy and priest rule?

The next day (May 31, 1863) an unusual stir was noticeable in the city. The air was all aglow with excitement. Horsemen were galloping in the streets leading pack-mules, and the sleepy town seemed full of bustle and animation. As we stood at our balcony, we saw many acquaintances, apparently equipped for a journey, speeding past, with a wave of the hand as a last farewell; and soon the attache of the American legation dropped in with a message from Mr. Corwin to the effect that President Juarez and his government were leaving the city.

The exodus of the previous night was thus explained. The remnants of General Comonfort's and General Ortega's armies had fallen back to serve as an escort for the government in its flight. The city was now without an administration, without a police, without an army. It was left unprotected, at the mercy of the mob or of the invader, and the serious question before us was how best to protect ourselves pending the arrival of the French forces.

The foreign representatives, fearing that the vanguard might be formed of the Mexican contingent under Marquez, and knowing the pitiless ferocity of the "Leopard," as the chieftain was called,* petitioned General Forey to send one of his divisions to take immediate possession of the capital. Meanwhile the foreign residents organized and formed themselves into mounted patrols, and although only seven hundred strong, they managed to maintain fair order.

* His name was Leonardo, from which came the sobriquet Leopardo.

Here and there ominous incidents occurred to show the necessity of such vigilance. A Frenchman was lassoed, and dragged through the streets by a small mob; another was shot in the head in front of our house, and, bleeding, took refuge in our patio. Upon inquiry, I was told that he had cried, "Vive la France!"

No one thought of retiring on that memorable night. From time to time a stray shot, a few shouting drunkards, or some other unwonted noise in the street, would excite our apprehension; then again, occasionally, some friend, passing with a patrol before our door, would step in and report that so far all was quiet.

Late that night, when at the window, listening in the stillness then reigning over the city, a distant but strangely familiar sound fell faintly upon my ear—very faintly; but never did the finest harmony born of Wagner's genius so fill a human soul with ecstasy. There was no mistaking it: it was a French bugle. The French were entering Mexico. We were safe, and now might go to bed.

IV. THE FRENCH IN THE CITY OF MEXICO—THE REGENCY

The next morning the town was swarming with red trousers, the wearers whereof were seeking quarters. From our balcony we saw, standing at the corner of the Calles de la Profesa and Espirito Santo, a little group of officers talking together in that half-earnest, half-distrait manner so characteristic of men newly landed in a town, whose interest in every trifle gets the better of the topic under immediate consideration.

By their uniforms and demeanor we could judge that one was a general and the others were officers of various rank. As we appeared at the balcony there was a perceptible flutter among them, and some of them began to ogle us as only Frenchmen could whose eyes had not rested upon a white woman for several months. This incident, trifling as it seems, was to become the key-note of our future Mexican existence. The group of officers in quest of suitable quarters turned out to be General Bazaine and his staff, some of whom afterward became our warm friends.

We now found another source of apprehension. The apartment we had rented, at the corner of the Calle de San Francisco, opposite the Iglesia de la Profesa, was larger than necessary for our small family, and a very spacious room looking upon Mexico's fashionable thoroughfare had been left unfurnished and unoccupied by us. It was obvious that we should be required to give it over for the use of some officer of the invading army, and the matter was naturally not without interest.

Early in the morning of June 5, a carriage drove up, and some middle-aged officers of the administration, in green-and-silver uniforms, applied for quarters. One of them was the paymaster-in-chief of the army, M. Ernest Louet. He was a worthy man, who afterward became a frequent visitor, although his general appearance and peculiar, peak-shaped skull, undisguised by any hirsute covering, were not likely favorably to impress frivolous feminine minds.*

* M. Louet, after the Franco-Prussian war, visited Marshal Bazaine in his Spanish retreat, and obtained from him all the documents relating to the intervention and the empire of Maximilian then in his possession. It was his intention to use them as the basis for an authentic history, which, however, he did not live to publish. The task thus begun by M. Louet was subsequently completed by M. Paul Gaulot, in 1889, under the title, "La Verite sur l'Expedition du Mexique, d'apres les Documents Inedits d'Ernest Louet, Payeur-en-Chef du Corps Expeditionnaire," and divided into three parts: "Un Reve d'Empire," "L'Empire de Maximilien," and "Fin d'Empire."

We drew a forlorn picture of the rooms, which, as a fact, were utterly unsuited to his purpose. He left without even looking at them, and we had a reprieve.

The unfinished condition of the apartments, as well as an abundant expenditure of tact and diplomacy on our part, saved us from other applicants, and we were beginning to flatter ourselves that we should escape this much-dreaded imposition when, late in the afternoon, two young naval officers called, accompanied by orderlies and pack-mules. They presented billets de logement, requesting to be given possession. We tried to discourage them, assuring them that the rooms contained no conveniences of any kind, not even furniture: but the young men were evidently easily satisfied; they politely but firmly insisted—their only wish, they said, being to camp under cover.

This annoyed us, and we showed them scant courtesy, not even attempting to disguise the fact that they were most unwelcome. Fate was, however, kind to us when it sent us these men. They turned out to be perfect gentlemen, and completely won us over by their unvarying good breeding under shabby treatment. Before long we were, and remained, the best of friends. As for their orderlies, they soon made love to our Indian maidens, and there is every reason to believe that the interlopers obtained all necessary comforts, after all. So all went well enough in the two menages.

Indeed, an entente cordiale between the population of Mexico and the French army was rapidly established. In a few days the place assumed an unwonted aspect of cheerfulness and festivity. The French officers, who for over a year past had led a life of hardship, were now bent upon pleasure.

They fell gracefully into the Mexican mode of life, and took kindly to the havanera, the bull-fights, the Paseo, and the style of flirtation preferred by the Mexican women. For this they soon coined a French word, noviotage,* and thus expressed the semi-Platonic love-making of indefinite duration and undefined limits which with the natives usually culminates in marriage, after a prolonged term of years, but which with foreigners seldom culminated at all, for lack of time. They "played the bear,"** and ogled their chosen one from the street or at the Alameda, or followed her carriage on horseback at the Paseo, according to the most approved Mexican methods; and in exchange for small favors received, they cast a glow of sparkling cheerfulness upon the dull city of Montezuma.

* Derived from novio, "betrothed lover."

** The Mexicans call hacer l'oso the mode of courtship by which the lover, on horseback, passes under his chosen one's window, up and down, casting longing glances at her—the worse the weather the more ardent the love.

General Forey made his triumphant entrance on June 10. It was a magnificent sight, and one not easily forgotten. As the victorious veteran troops,—many of whom had seen the Crimea, Syria, and Italy,—in their battered though scrupulously neat uniforms, marched through the Calle de San Francisco, laden with their cumbersome campaign outfit, the whole population turned out to see them, and the balconies and windows on the line of march were lined with eager and interested faces.

This was no ordinary pageant. It was serious work, and full of the deepest meaning. These survivors of an army of thirty thousand men had arduously fought their way to this triumph for sixteen months. No one will probably ever know how many of their comrades had dropped on the roadside; and the weather-beaten faces, bronzed by long exposure to the tropical sun, the patched clothes, the long line of ambulances following in the rear, told a story in which little room was left for the imagination. The sight kindled genuine interest and aroused the sympathy of the crowd, and something very like spontaneous enthusiasm thrilled through the air on their passage.

The keys of the city had been solemnly offered to General Forey by General Salas, amid the acclamations of the people. The next day M. de Saligny presented a list of thirty-five citizens destined to form a junta. These were to select three men to act as regents pending the final decision of the people with regard to a permanent form of government. The junta was empowered to add to its numbers two hundred and fifteen citizens, supposed to be taken from all classes, who, with the thirty-five appointed by the French, would compose the assembly of notables upon whom must devolve the carrying out of the farce which it was intended must take the place of a popular expression of the will of the country.

Don Theodosio Lares was elected its president. This junta, in a secret meeting at which two hundred and thirty-one members were present, deliberated upon the form of government to be chosen for the Mexican nation and on July 10, at a public meeting, presented a report in which the republican system was denounced as the cause of the greatest evils which had of late years been the scourge of the country, and monarchy was advocated as the only remedy.

Four articles were voted upon, with only two dissenting voices: (1) The nation adopts as a form of government a constitutional monarchy, hereditary under a Catholic prince. (2) The sovereign will take the title of Emperor of Mexico. (3) The imperial crown of Mexico is offered to his Royal Highness Prince Ferdinand Maximilian, Archduke of Austria, for himself and his descendants. (4) In the case where, owing to unforeseen circumstances, the Archduke Ferdinand Maximilian should not take possession of the throne offered him, the Mexican government trusts in the good will of his Majesty Emperor Napoleon III to designate another Catholic prince to whom the crown shall be offered. A regency, composed of General Almonte, General Salas, and Archbishop Labastida, was forthwith established, under the protection of the French.

It was obvious to all that the performance was enacted for the "benefit of the gallery." Gossip even told how the French had paid for the very clothes worn by some of the so-called "notables" upon that occasion. Nevertheless, the monarchy, by the will of the people, was voted in, and a commission was appointed, consisting of the most distinguished among the reactionary leaders, to wait upon Maximilian of Austria, and to offer him the throne on behalf of the Mexican nation.

But although the part played by the French in this comedy was thinly disguised, every one in the capital was now in a good humor. After the severe strain of the past year, the onerous burdens which had been imposed upon the people by the Liberal government in order to carry on the war,—the forced loans raised from the wealthy, the leva by means of which the poor were seized upon and pressed into the army,—a sudden reprieve had come. All responsibility now seemed lifted off the Mexican people and assumed by the French; and the revival of trade under the impulse given by the influx of pleasure-loving foreigners, who freely spent their money, was regarded as an earnest of the prosperity to come. No one seemed disposed to be over-critical as to methods, if only peace and plenty could be assured.

It would seem, however, that Napoleon's instructions to General Forey had not been exactly carried out. According to these, and in order to retain full control of political operations, the general was himself to appoint the provisional government, with General Almonte at its head. After this, tranquillity having been established in the country, he was to call for a popular vote to decide upon the form of government to be adopted and to constitute a national congress.*

*See official letters, November 1, December 17, 1862, February 14, 1863.

The French government had repeatedly declared to England and to the world that "no government would be imposed upon the Mexican people." Had it been honest when signing the provisions of the treaty of London, and later those of the convention of La Soledad, the armed expedition had now reached its end. Indeed, quite enough had already happened to show the French statesmen how illusory had been the promises of the Mexican refugees and the representations of Messrs. de Saligny and Jecker; and now, once more and for the last time, the opportunity was offered Napoleon gracefully to withdraw with the honors of war from the fool's errand on which he had so recklessly embarked.

The French army was now in Mexico. The commander-in-chief and the French minister might dictate their terms to the enemy from his fallen capital, and then retrace their steps homeward.

But this was not to be; unwilling to recognize his own error, Napoleon III preferred attributing to the mismanagement of his agents the difficulties that had sprung up on every side, and he resolved to persevere in his original intention. As for General Forey, whether his dullness of perception failed to grasp the true drift of his master's mind, or whether he was unable to steer his way through the tortuous policy which he was called upon to further, he seemed to regard his mission as fulfilled. After he had established the native provisional government, he complacently rested in the enjoyment of his new title of Marshal of France, apparently overlooking the fact that outside of the capital the national party held the country as absolutely as ever. He issued a decree confiscating the property of all Liberals who did not lay down their arms, and allowed the regency, which was composed of three clerical leaders,—General Almonte, of whom Marshal Bazaine was wont to say that he meant well, but il se prend trop au serieux, General Salas, a conservative old fossil unearthed for the occasion, and Archbishop Labastida,—to foreshadow an era of reaction and retrogression.

A decree (1863) intended to stop the exporting of gold, and another confiscating the property of political adversaries, created so much uneasiness that the French government was obliged to interfere and enforce their repeal. An ordinance compelling every one to kneel in the street upon the passage of the eucharist created loud dissatisfaction among the liberal-minded; and ordinances forbidding work on Sunday without the permission of the parish priest, and suspending work in the erection of buildings upon land formerly belonging to the clergy, had eventually to be repealed.

Religious processions had been forbidden by the Liberal government. One of the first mistakes made by the commander-in-chief was to allow the clergy to celebrate in June the Fete-Dieu, that should have been celebrated in May, but had been omitted, as Juarez was then in possession of the city. Not only did General Forey consent to this, but he and his officers attended the procession, an act which excited the sarcasm of the Liberals and gave substance to the fear that the French protectorate meant reaction.

The priests and clericals fully believed that their turn to govern had come. They actually notified the tenants of former clergy property not to pay rent to their landlords, as the sales of such property had been the work of Satan, and were now to be annulled, and that if they paid their rent they must eventually be called upon to pay it over again to the church, the rightful owner.

Meanwhile Maximilian's faith had been shaken by the refusal of England to guarantee the empire. When, in the autumn of 1861, the negotiations secretly carried on with regard to the establishment of a Mexican monarchy had at last assumed a tangible form, and serious propositions had been made to the Archduke Maximilian by M. Gutierrez de Estrada (the representative of the reactionary party in Mexico, acting at the instigation of Napoleon III), the archduke, with the approval of his brother Emperor Francis Joseph, had acquiesced under two principal conditions: "(1) The support, not only moral, but material and efficient, of the two great powers (France and England); (2) the clearly expressed wish of the Mexican people."*

* See note drawn up under his supervision by his secretary, the Baron de Pont, bearing date September 27, 1861, published in "La Verite sur l'Expedition du Mexique," loc. cit., pp. 8, 9, and compare M. de Keratry, "L'Empereur Maximilien," etc., pp. 8, 9. It has been said that the project was submitted to Maximilian three years before the treaty of Miramar was signed (see Charles d'Hericault, "Maximilien et le Mexique," p. 23), and I heard it asserted, while in Mexico, that the Mexican empire was not wholly unconnected with the peace of Villafranca, after which the archduke had retired to his castle on the Adriatic. However this may be, the above shows that official, though secret, negotiations were opened with regard to Maximilian's future empire even before the treaty of London was signed (October 31, 1861), and that, in entering into the triple alliance, England was being led by her wily ally further than she meant to go.

French diplomacy had failed in its efforts to secure British concurrence. Maximilian now showed himself unwilling to regard the invitation of the junta assembled in the capital as sufficient to constitute a claim to the imperial crown. He insisted upon a similar expression of feeling from the other large centers of population in the country, and stated his readiness to accept the trust "when the vast territory should have been pacified." This meant the conquest of the country, neither more nor less.

Napoleon apparently did not hesitate. Trusting in the love of warlike achievement so strong in the French people, he pushed ahead along his dangerous path. That even now he clung to the practicability of his original plan is shown by the almost naive manner in which, on September 12,1863, he wrote to General Bazaine that "the PRINCIPAL object at present was to pacify and organize (!)" the country by calling upon all men of good will to rally around the new order of things and by preventing the enactment of reactionary measures. He then still hoped and believed that the return to France of the outlay caused by the expedition could be guaranteed by means of a great loan raised in Mexico—WHEN, organized and restored to prosperity. He constantly urged upon his agents the organization of the finances of the country and of the Mexican army.

Immediately upon the arrival of the French, Napoleon had sent a financier, M. Budin, to put order into the country's resources. M. Budin was a commonplace, middle-aged little man, of mediocre ability, whose personality was not calculated to impress one with an idea of intellectual force. I was told, by those who were in a position to judge of his ability as a specialist, that, although a first-class administrative officer, he was lacking in initiative, and was in no way qualified to extricate Mexico from financial difficulties. His attainments were those acquired in the daily routine of an upper clerk's well-defined duties, and his mind was of narrow scope, ill fitted to adapt itself to the entirely new problems set before it. He had been Paymaster of the French army during the Crimean and the Italian wars, and afterward receveur-general de la Savoie. He brought with him a mining engineer and a staff of custom-house and revenue officers.

He did not distinguish himself, one of his earliest acts being to urge the promulgation of the above-mentioned decree sequestrating the property of all who were then opposed to the new order of things. He also reinstated the old method of administering justice, which was a disappointment to the progressive element. To be sure, Maximilian, upon his arrival, treated him coldly, and did not help him to make a success of his mission. His place was successively filled by M. de Maintenant and by M. Corta, who were not more successful in bringing the revenues of the empire up to its requirements. M. de Bonnefons, a fourth financier, sent in 1865, fell ill and was compelled to return to France. The year following his arrival, he, in turn, was replaced by M. Langlais.

On July 16, 1863, the Emperor had promoted General Forey to the rank of marshal, and had thus softened the recall of his incompetent, though faithful, servant.

The newly made marshal celebrated this promotion by a ball, at which a trifling incident occurred which made an impression upon me, and which, no doubt, General Forey remembered for some time. He was a very heavy man, of full habit, tall, with a short neck and red complexion, all the more ruddy by contrast with his gray hair and mustache. While waltzing past the general, I saw the light chair upon which he sat suddenly give way with a loud crash under his ponderous weight, and down came the commander-in-chief hard upon the floor. Rumors of his probable downfall were already reaching us, and the appositeness of the situation appealed to us. I jokingly whispered to my partner, a young officer on his staff: "Mon general, vous avez fait la culbute." We both thoughtlessly laughed, and were caught in the act by his Excellency at the moment when, helped to his feet, unhurt, by the bystanders, he was endeavoring to veil under an assumption of increased dignity his consciousness of the absurdity of the accident. He flushed up angrily, and, I was afterward told, never quite forgave the young man for his share in our disrespectful mirth.

He was most unpopular. His whole conduct, since his arrival in Mexico, had been characterized by weakness, indecision, and lack of judgment, and he had shown himself in every respect unequal to the difficult task before him. Colonel Loizillon says that, on the way to Puebla, when the generals assembled in council of war differed, instead of deciding the question the commander-in-chief would adjourn, beseechingly saying: "Mon Dieu, tachez donc de vous entendre"* ("Gentlemen, DO try to come to an understanding"). He had allowed himself to be deceived by the French minister to Mexico with the glaring facts before his eyes. As a military chief, his procrastination had given the Mexicans the time they needed fully to organize their defense; and had it not been for General Bazaine's energy and military capacity in urging and successfully carrying out the attack upon the fort of San Xavier, the siege of Puebla, already prolonged far beyond the limits of all likelihood, might have cost the French a still greater expenditure of time and human life. Indeed, it was the openly expressed opinion of many French officers that to famine was principally due the fall of Puebla. "Sans cela nous y serions encore," they would say.

* "Lettres sur l'Expedition du Mexique," p. 101.

General Forey's elevation had been due mainly to the fact that he was one of the men who had served Napoleon in 1851 in the coup d'etat. Indeed, many of the Emperor's most glaring failures were due to the same cause,—i.e., loyalty to individuals,—which led him to place in responsible positions men of small merit and of less principle who had stood by Caesar and his fortunes.

In France the effect of the general's incapacity had been serious. The delay that had occurred in bringing about a result announced as easy of accomplishment had furnished sharp weapons to the opposition. It had forced the government to ask the Chamber of Deputies for large appropriations to conduct the war upon a serious scale. It was no longer a military parade from Vera Cruz to Mexico to present the French flag to the enthusiastic gratitude of the Mexicans: it was a fighting army of thirty-five thousand men to be maintained across the seas at the expense of France.

The French leaders may be said to have displayed, in their Mexican venture, the same lack of administrative efficiency and of military organization, the same insufficient knowledge of and preparation for the task to be performed, as so conspicuously appeared at the very outset of the Franco-Prussian War. It is impossible to read the accounts of the various campaigns since published without recognizing the presence, in victory over an unorganized enemy, of the elements of the later failure when the same men were arrayed against the strongly organized German forces.*

* It is interesting, in this connection, to find that the same conditions existed in France at the time of the Crimean war. General Bosquet, one of the heroes of that expedition, in his letters constantly denounced the administration for its lack of preparation. Under date of January 14, 1854, he says: "Imagine that they have not yet made any preparation. The cavalry has neither horses nor men; neither has the artillery. No orders have been given about harness, or about any new material." And in another letter, written on the eve of his departure for the seat of war, he repeats the same complaints. Marshal St. Arnaud, the commander-in-chief, wrote from Gallipoli to the Emperor that the army lacked the very necessaries of life: "One cannot make war," he said in a note dated May 27, "without bread, shoes, kettles, and water-cans."

With characteristic patriotism, the Chamber voted the appropriations necessary to vindicate the honor of the French flag; but the government was condemned to hear many unpleasant truths.

As for M. de Saligny, he had turned the French legation into a business office, in which the guaranty of France was traded upon to cover the most doubtful transactions. Napoleon had at last recognized his true character, and now—too late, alas!—recalled him from his post. "De gre ou de force, quand memo il aurait donne sa demission," he had written to General Bazaine.*

* November 1, 1863. See Louet, loc. cit., "Un Reve d'Empire," p. 208.

But this unforeseen contingency greatly disturbed the French minister in his operations. His accomplices, the clerical leaders and others, worked for him, and moved heaven and earth to have his recall reconsidered. They failed; but to make up for his disappointment the Mexican National Assembly voted him a national reward of one hundred thousand dollars. Although Marshal

Forey had not yet left the country, General Bazaine remonstrated with General Almonte, who, however, resented his interference.

Both M. de Saligny and Marshal Forey enjoyed too much playing the leading role to depart willingly. They lingered on, much to the amusement of the onlookers, until General Bazaine grew impatient at the awkwardness of his own position. The ridiculous side of the complication was seized upon by the wags of the army; bets were taken, and a song the refrain of which was, "Partiront-ils, partiront-ils pas," was popularly sung everywhere, the innumerable verses of which showed the inexhaustible interest taken in the subject.*

* Plus rapide que l'eclair
Un bruit circule en ville;
La joie, la gaiete sont dans l'air;
On s'aborde, on babille;
Soldats et pekins
Se serrent la main
En disant, 'Quelle chance!'
Tout bas on redit,
Forey, Saligny
Sont rappeles en France,"
etc.

PART III

THE EMPIRE OF MAXIMILIAN I 1864-65

I. MARSHAL BAZAINE

In October, 1863, the reins of power, so loosely held by General Forey, at last passed into firmer hands. General Bazaine took command of affairs. It was high time. The Juarists, profiting by the long respite afforded them, were reorganizing in the interior, and were threatening. The daily stage was attacked on its way to the coast as often as not. Highwaymen tore up the rails of the Paso del Macho Railroad, attacked the train, and killed passengers. Detachments of banditti, called by courtesy guerrillas, everywhere infested the roads, even at the very gates of the capital. A picnic was given to us at this time, by some officers of General Bazaine's staff, at a wild, beautiful spot, where the ruins of a graceful aqueduct, built by the Spaniards, formed the principal attraction. It was less than a twenty-mile ride, yet it was deemed unsafe to go without a strong escort, although we and the officers who gave the affair formed, with their orderlies, a large cavalcade.

General Forey's policy in letting the regency have its way, and in countenancing reactionary legislation of an aggressive character, had discouraged the honest partizans of order. The clergy now openly declared that Maximilian was pledged to the holy see for the restoration of the confiscated property of the clergy to its original owners. The archbishop, newly landed, did all that was in his power to encourage such a belief and to guide the regency to an uncompromising surrender to the holy see.* As the security of immense transactions in clergy property was involved, serious uneasiness was felt.

* Compare M. de Keratry, loc. cit., p. 31.

General Bazaine handled all these complications with firmness and skill. He compelled the regency to repeal the decrees most objectionable to the thinking portion of the community. He enforced the maintaining of all bona-fide transactions in clergy property, but advocated the revision of such contracts as might be proved fraudulent, and urged a concordat proposing that the state provide for the support of the clergy. His orders were to rally around him the Liberal chiefs, and he strove by a wise, tactful policy to conciliate men of all shades of opinion. His vigorous military action soon established order in the territory surrounding Mexico. With the concurrence of General Almonte, who earnestly wished the welfare of his country, he reduced Archbishop Labastida to terms, if not to silence.

Having done this, he took the field, concentrated his army from the various distant points where the different corps had been ordered in view of the campaign which he was preparing, and within six weeks defeated, by rapid and well-concerted blows, Generals Doblado, Negrete, Comonfort, and Uraga, who at that time, thanks to General Forey's procrastination, were holding the country with. the rallied forces of the Liberal party.

From Morelia to San Luis, from Mexico to Guadalajara, the French flag waved over every stronghold. The conquered cities received the conquerors coldly, but acknowledged the archduke (of whom, we were told by the officers, many did not even know the name) just as resignedly as for over forty years of civil war they had been wont to acknowledge the victor's chosen presidential candidate.

This campaign was little more than a race, and it was said that the French conquered the country with their legs far more than with their bayonets.

In February, 1864, the general, uneasy at the turn which political affairs were taking in the capital, returned with an escort as suddenly as he had departed. It was high time. In his absence, Mgr. Labastida, not giving due consideration to the change of leadership that had taken place at the French headquarters, had so far forgotten himself as to fulminate, in the name of the church, against the French. But upon the return of the commander-in-chief he reconsidered his action, and publicly "gave them his blessing."*

* M. de Keratry, loc. cit., p. 33.

General Bazaine was at this time the most popular man in the army. Hitherto eminently successful in all his military undertakings, he had risen from the ranks, having won his honors step by step upon the battle-field, at first by his courage, later by his remarkable military ability.

He was a plain-looking man, short and thick-set, whose plebeian features one might search in vain for a spark of genius or a ray of imagination; and yet under the commonplace exterior dwelt a kindly spirit, an intelligence of no mean order, and, despite a certain coarseness of thought and expression too common among Frenchmen, a soul upon which the romance of life had impressed its mark in lines of fire.

The story went that, when a colonel, he had in Spain come across a little girl of great beauty and personal attractions, who seemed to him out of place amid her surroundings. He picked up the little wild rose as it grew on the roadside, and conceived the notion of transplanting it into good, rich soil, and of giving it its share of sunshine. He took the child to Paris, where he left her in a convent to be educated.

The soldier continued his brilliant career in the Crimea, Italy, Syria, and Africa; and when, after some years, he returned to Paris, he found the little girl grown into a beautiful and attractive woman, whose heart was full of warm gratitude for her benefactor. He fell in love with her, and, breaking through all rules of French matrimonial usage, married her.

Her charm won for her many friends in the circle which his position entitled her to enter; her attractions exposed her to temptations which her early training had ill fitted her to meet; and her death, which occurred under peculiarly distressing circumstances soon after his promotion to the command of the army in Mexico, was a cruel blow. The news of his loss reached the general while away from the capital on the brilliant campaign which added the greater part of the country to the projected empire (November, 1863). After a funeral mass, which he heard with his officers, he retired to his tent, and, alone, fought that hardest of all battles, and conquered his own heart. In a few days he returned to his duty, and no one ever knew what had passed in his innermost soul.

Two years later a ball was given at the quartier-general. Bazaine, who had lately been promoted to the rank of marshal (1864), had stopped for a moment to say a few words, when one of his guests, a young Mexican girl who was waltzing by, suddenly stopped near us, having torn her dress. Pins were produced, the damaged ruffle was repaired, and the girl passed on. "Who is this?" asked the marshal, evidently much struck with her appearance. "It is extraordinary," he muttered, "how much she reminds me of my wife." He looked distrait, and shortly after excused himself, and wandered off in the direction Mlle. de la Pena had taken.

The courtship was a short one. Maximilian, in order to facilitate a union which he deemed to be in the interest of his government, gave the young girl as a dowry the palace of San Cosme,* valued at one hundred thousand dollars; and thus was May united, to December. Two children were born to the marshal, one of them in Mexico,** and never was father prouder of his young wife and of her offspring than was the marshal.***

* A suburb west of Mexico.

** Maximilian was his godfather,

*** When, after the Franco-Prussian war, the marshal, having been made a sacrifice to France's wounded pride, was court-martialed, and, amid the imprecations of his countrymen, was imprisoned in the Fort de Ste. Marguerite, his young wife and her cousin contrived the perilous escape of the old man. By means of a rope procured for him by them he lowered himself from the walls of the fortress. Mme. Bazaine was awaiting him in a small boat, the oars of which were held by her cousin. A ship was near by, ready to sail, on which they sought refuge in Spain. And so it was that a fallen marshal of France passed from a state prison into exile, where he ended a life in which fame and romance had an equal share.

II. A BED OF ROSES IS A GOLD-MINE

The difficult task intrusted to General Bazaine had been triumphantly performed.

The adhesion of the main part of Mexico to the empire was secured. Oajaca and Guerrero, in the south, still held out, under General Porfirio Diaz, and in the north Chihuahua and Durango had not submitted; but enough of the Mexican territory was pacified to answer immediate purposes. European criticism and the scruples of Maximilian must be satisfied by this appearance of a popular election and a quasi-universal suffrage. For forty years Mexico had not been so quiet. The defeated and demoralized Liberal forces were scattered, and the Juarez government, retreating toward the extreme northern frontier at Monterey, seemed to have nothing left save its eternal rights.

On May 28, 1864, Maximilian of Austria and the Archduchess Charlotte reached Vera Cruz on the Austrian frigate Novara. They were escorted by the French man-of war Themis, By some unfortunate contretemps, the deputation that had left the capital with much pomp and flutter in order to greet them was not there. They arrived as ordinary passengers, the people evincing little curiosity and less cordiality, as we have seen. Vera Cruz is in itself not calculated to cheer the newcomer, and their first impression of their venture was a painful one.

In due time, however, things righted themselves. General Almonte and his suite appeared upon the scene, and all the necessary pageant was brought into play to soothe the wounded feelings of the new sovereigns. They landed on the following day at six o'clock in the morning. The early hour interfered with any effective popular demonstration, and their reception, as they proceeded to Loma Alta, at that time the terminus of the railroad, was by no means a brilliant one. At this point they took carriages and drove on, escorted by a body of cavalry commanded by General Galvez and Colonel Miguel Lopez. Near the Cerro del Chiquihuite the imperial carriage broke down, and the young sovereigns had to accept that of General de Maussion. It was in the midst of a terrible tropical storm, which put out the torches with which their escort lighted the way, that the imperial cortege entered Cordoba. Here, however, they were met by a crowd of torch-bearing Indians, whose enthusiasm made up for the gloom and disappointments which had hitherto marked their arrival.

The rest of the journey was a well-prepared ovation. The priests, now eager to come to the fore, had ordered out the Indian population. The action of Maximilian in going to Rome, and in piously securing the papal blessing before sailing to take possession of his new dominions, had been received by the ultra-clerical party as a hopeful symptom of returning papal ascendancy under the coming reign.*

* On April 19, 1864, Maximilian and the archduchess had repaired to Rome in order, said the official papers, to "implore the benediction of the august chief of the church, and to place their future effort under the aegis of his paternal intercession and of his powerful authority." The sermon preached by Pius IX in the Sistine Chapel on April 29, in which the Holy Father encouraged the new sovereigns to accomplish the designs of Providence in a mission which was but a part of a "grand scheme of Christian propagandism," linked the empire to the clerical party.

At this time Napoleon III could no longer be unaware that the recognition of the liberty of religious worship, of toleration, and of the reform laws promulgated by Juarez, was a necessity of the situation, and that the church could not be reinstated as in the past. His representatives in Mexico knew that the reactionary platform was not only an unsafe one, but an impossible one for the empire to stand upon in Mexico; and they were endeavoring to extricate themselves from the consequences of their faux pas with as much dignity and consistency as circumstances would admit. The awkwardness of the situation was, therefore, only added to by this demonstration of piety and filial obedience on the part of the new Mexican rulers. Yet it had the effect of rallying the clergy for the time being, who did their best to increase their claims by a public display of devotion to the empire.

The new sovereigns might well imagine that they were the elect of the people when, followed by a multitude of Indians, they entered the capital.

It was under the scorching rays of a hot June sun that they made their formal entry into the city of Montezuma.* Never had such a sight been seen since the days of the Aztecs. The lavish ingenuity of the French—anxious, for obvious reasons, to make the occasion a telling one—vied with the interested patriotism of the clerical party to excite the enthusiasm of the people, and to produce an impression upon the Austrian travelers. Triumphal arches of verdure, draped with flags and patriotic devices, were raised along the principal avenues leading to the Plaza Mayor and to the palace. As far as the eye could reach, the festively decked windows, the streets, and the flat roofs of the houses were crowded with people eager to catch a glimpse of the new sovereigns. As they slowly approached in the official landau, the crowd was so dense as to be with difficulty held back.

* June 12, 1864. The Archduchess Charlotte was born in Brussels on June 7, 1840, and she was then twenty-four years old. The archduke was born at Schonbrunn on July 6, 1832, and was therefore not quite thirty-two years of age.

It was a singular spectacle. They seemed so tall and fair, these two young people of another race, as they smilingly advanced through the swarthy multitude of their small, ragged subjects, bowing in acknowledgment of their acclamations! Involuntarily one thought of visiting angels, or, better still, of the fair god Quetzalcohuatl, whom the Mexican legend of olden times brought from the East to rule over and to civilize the natives of this land by bringing them plenty. The analogy spontaneously occurred to every thoughtful onlooker, and spread like lightning throughout the city.

Dramatic as it might be, the situation was not without its comic touches. Some one in the imperial entourage had the unfortunate idea of imitating for the Emperor's body-guard the sky-blue-and-silver uniform of Napoleon's tall Cent-Gardes. It is hard to imagine anything more amusing than the caricature thus produced of the French picked regiment, which saw the light for the first time on that occasion.

It was at first difficult to establish among the republican Mexicans the rigid etiquette of the Austrian court, and some unsuccessful attempts to do so were fruitful of heartache on both sides. For instance, when Senora Salas, the wife of the regent, was first introduced to her young sovereign, the poor little old lady amiably advanced, prepared to give her the national abraso—a graceful greeting which closely simulates an embrace. In Mexico its significance in good society was very much that of a shake of the hand with us. Much to her consternation, the tall Empress stepped back and drew herself up to her full height at what she regarded an undue liberty, while tears of indignation came into her eyes. Whereupon the poor senora was dissolved in tears, and the incident came near to disturbing the good feeling that every one hoped might at once be established between the sovereigns and their Mexican court.

For a brief space we all felt as though a new era were indeed about to dawn upon this Western land. There is no doubt that at this time the empire seemed a fact, and that, with the exception of a certain number of outlying districts, the country was fast rallying around its banner. It represented order and stability, while the Liberals occupied the position of anarchists.*

* See Masseras, "Un Essai d'Empire au Mexique," p. 9, where he quotes a letter addressed by Senor Zamacona to President Juarez, and bearing date June 16, 1864.

General Bazaine did all in his power to inaugurate brilliantly the advent of the empire. A splendid ball was given to the young sovereigns at the quartier-general—such a ball as is seldom seen outside the great European capitals. The general's aides-de-camp had been put in charge, and all that unlimited funds and a large experience of such matters could accomplish was done to make the occasion the memorable feature of a memorable historic event.

The great patio of the palace of San Cosme was floored and roofed over to serve as a ball-room. At the back of the great arcade surrounding it, the arches and pillars of which were draped with French and Mexican flags, was banked a profusion of plants and flowers, upon which was cast the light of myriads of candles and colored lanterns. In the middle of the huge improvised ball-room the great fountain played, and its sparkling waters were seen through masses of tropical vegetation. Here and there enormous warlike trophies reminded the spectator that he was the guest of a great army. The artillery had supplied groups of heavy cannon, stacked on end, and huge piles of cannon-balls, while at intervals trophies of flags and drums, of guns and bayonets, tastefully grouped about the French and the Mexican coats of arms, broke with striking effect the expanse of wall above the arcades.

When the imperial cortege entered the crowded ball-room, the quadrille d'honneur was danced by their Majesties, the general-in-chief, and the more distinguished members of their respective suites, after which the Emperor and Empress were respectfully escorted by the general to their throne, set under a crimson-velvet canopy resting upon French cannon.

They were so young and so handsome in their imperial pomp! By them stood Princess Zichy, tall and distinguished, in a simple white-tulle gown and natural flowers, with a wealth of such diamonds as are seldom seen on one person—a homely woman, but interesting to us as the daughter of the Metternichs. Her husband, Prince Zichy, was the most striking figure in the imperial party. He wore the full state costume of a Hungarian Magyar; and his many orders, hanging around his neck and upon his breast, as well as the marvelous hilt, belt, and jeweled sheath of his ancestral sword, stood out finely upon his black-velvet costume, and made him a conspicuous figure even in an assemblage where the ordinary evening dress was almost unseen.

The glitter of all this court life, the revival of trade, the abundance of money so freely brought and spent in the country, dazzled the people, and a golden dust was thrown into the eyes of all, which for a brief period prevented them from seeing the true drift of political events. Indeed, the brilliancy of the scene was not entirely due to flash-light. The revenues derived from the customs of Tampico and Vera Cruz were at this time materially increasing. An official report, read to the French Chamber in 1865, showed that the revenues from those ports, which for three months in 1864 had been $96,000 and $900,000 respectively, had for the same period in 1865 risen respectively to $431,000 and $1,645,000.

Large concessions for railroads had been asked for and granted under solid guaranties—the line from Vera Cruz to Mexico to an Anglo-French company, pledged to complete it in five years, and another concession for three lines, for the carrying out of which $4,500,000 had been subscribed.

Telegraph lines were being established; coal, petroleum, and gold- and silver-mines were being exploited, or were in a fair way to be.

The good management of the regency under General Almonte's frugal administration had accumulated a balance of 15,000,000 francs in the treasury—a small surplus which must have been encouraging to the Emperor upon his arrival. Moreover, the loan of 200,000,000 francs, so readily taken up abroad, had given a substantial foundation for hopeful anticipation, and it seemed as though France might possibly get out of her rash venture with honor and profit.

The mirage that had lured Napoleon to these perilous shores now appeared materially nearer, and its outlines seemed more vivid and attractive than ever before.

But it was an easy matter to create an empire as the result of an armed invasion of an unwilling land, it was quite another thing to organize it upon a permanent basis. As Prince Napoleon—familiarly known as Plon-Plon—very wittily remarked later, "One can do anything with bayonets, except sit upon them." ("On peut tout faire avec des baionnettes, excepte s'asseoir dessus.") For over two years Napoleon III endeavored to make Maximilian perform the latter feat—with what result we all know only too well.

III. THORNS

The details of Maximilian's court once settled, and the code of etiquette to be used adopted, the new sovereign started forth upon a tour of the provinces, to present himself to the loyalty of his subjects. The Empress remained as regent, to govern under the guidance of the Commander-in-chief. Ovations had everywhere been prepared, and a semblance of popularity, so dear to Maximilian's heart, was the result. But immense sums were expended, and more precious time was wasted.

Upon his return, Mexican society turned out en masse to do him honor. We all sallied forth in a monster cavalcade by the Paseo de la Vega to meet him some miles out of the city, and escort him back to the palace. All this was pleasant and exciting, but wise heads saw that this was no time for idle pleasure, and some impatience was manifested at this pageantry.

Then began a series of administrative experiments. Many projects were mapped out with a view to placing Mexico abreast of the most advanced countries of the civilized world.

Among other premature efforts made at this time, when the young Emperor gave fullest flight to his dreams, was a Department of the Navy. Nothing could more clearly demonstrate how whimsical was the mind of the Austrian ex-admiral and how slight was his grasp of the situation. Long-postponed issues, involving vital questions of policy and of administration, were awaiting his decision, and he busied himself with frivolities and with impossibilities. These early days gave the keynote of his three years' reign.

Captain Destroyat, a French naval officer, was made secretary of the navy. As the Mexican government did not own a canoe, and as there was at that time no serious likelihood of its ever owning a battle-ship, this sinecure caused no little merriment among us, and many were the practical jokes of which the hapless cabinet officer was the victim.

His quarters were situated one block below our house, in the Calle de Espiritu Santo. This street, owing to a depression in the level and to bad drainage, was usually flooded, during the rainy season, after every severe aguacero. So impassable did it then become that even men were compelled to engage the services of a cargador to carry them across "pickaback." When came the first shower after his new dignity had been conferred upon Captain Destroyat, his comrades, bent upon fun, purchased a toy flotilla, which they floated, flying the Mexican flag, down the street. In mock dignity the tiny ships came to an anchor before his door, much to every one's merriment, excepting, it was whispered, to that of the powers that were, who found a sting in the harmless levity.*

* The new Navy Department, although substantial advances were made to it by the French treasury for the purpose of guarding the coast against smugglers, did little to justify its existence. Two years later, when Empress Charlotte arrived in Vera Cruz, about to sail for Europe on that the fruitless errand from which she was never to return, there was not one rowboat flying the Mexican flag ready to convey her to the steamer which was lying in port at anchor. A boat belonging to a French man-of-war was placed at her disposal, but the unfortunate woman, then embittered by the treatment received at the hands of the French government, flatly refused to be taken, even over so short a distance, under the French flag; and the incident gave rise to a painful scene. As the Empress was then on her way as a suppliant to the court of the Tuileries, there is every reason to believe this illogical and almost childish sensitiveness was one of the first symptoms of the cerebral derangement that was so soon to become evident. Other exhibitions of an impaired judgment were related which then seemed incomprehensible.

Maximilian has been uniformly blamed by French writers for frittering away the first precious months of his reign in dreams, or in the settlement of minor details, the triviality of which was in glaring contrast with the gravity of the issues before him. True as this criticism may be in theory, it is perhaps to be regretted—if we consider his Majesty's youth and inexperience, and his absolute ignorance of the conditions which he was called upon to face, as well as of the capabilities and personal history of the men with whom he was to deal—that he did not longer continue to allow others, who had painfully earned a clearer knowledge of the situation, to rule in his name. The French, after a long series of preliminary blunders, were just beginning to understand the country when the Emperor arrived and attempted independently to acquire the same lesson, at the expense of the nation, of his party, and of his allies.

It soon became obvious that the young monarch was not equal to the task which he had undertaken, and a feeling of disappointment prevailed. Unendowed with the force and clearness of mind necessary in an organizer, he nevertheless insisted upon all administrative work passing through his own imperial bureau. At the head of this bureau he placed an obscure personal favorite, a Belgian named Eloin, who had risen to favor through his social accomplishments. This man did not speak one word of Spanish, hated the French, despised the Mexicans, and was more ignorant than his master himself of American questions in general, and of Mexican affairs in particular.

While in office he used his power to repress much of the impulse given to enterprise by the French. His narrow views were responsible for a jealous policy which excluded all that he could not personally appreciate and manage. He and the Emperor undertook to decide questions upon which they were then hardly competent to give an intelligent opinion. The Mexican leaders were made to feel that they had no influence, the French that they had no rights. A chill was suddenly felt to pervade the official atmosphere. As a prominent member of the Belgian legation once remarked:

"To eat priest for breakfast and Frenchman for dinner, when one has been called to the throne by the clergy, and must rely upon France for sole support, may be regarded as a dangerous policy." After doing much mischief, M. Eloin was sent abroad upon a mysterious mission. It was rumored that he had gone to watch over his master's personal interests abroad.*

* On December 28,1864, Maximilian entered a protest against the family compact exacted from him by his brother, the Emperor Francis Joseph, on April 9, a few days before his departure from Miramar and communicated to the Reichsrath on November 16th. In this curious document he stated that it was upon the suggestion of the Emperor of Austria that the throne of Mexico had been offered to him; that after the negotiations were closed, when his withdrawal must have brought about the most serious European complications, the Emperor Francis Joseph, accompanied by his most intimate councilors, had come hastily to Miramar to force from him an absolute renunciation of his birthrights; that, having given his word to the Mexican delegation sent to offer him a throne, he had signed this unqualifiable compact, but that experienced diplomats and expert jurists,

after studying the question, were of the opinion that a document exacted under such conditions was null and void; and that the diets, with the consent of the two interested emperors, were alone competent to decide upon such rights. In this case the diets had not even been consulted.

This protest, the text of which is published in M. Domenech's "Histoire du Mexique" (vol. iii, p. 204), excited the suspicion that Maximilian had not relinquished his European ambitions, and that the role of Liberal ruler which he played upon the Mexican stage was played partly to an Austrian audience.

A few months after this (May 3, 1865) M. Eloin was sent abroad, ostensibly to treat of a new loan; he was no financier, and it is likely that his mission was a confidential one, the political nature of which comes out clearly in the intercepted letter, under date of September 27, 1866, which was published in the United States. (See p. 243.)

Indeed, the presence of the personal friends and countrymen of the sovereigns who had accompanied them in their voluntary exile caused a note of discord in the general harmony of the first days of the empire, indicative of the cacophony which was soon to follow. Prince and Princess Zichy and Countess Collonitz soon returned home, but a number of men remained to occupy lucrative and confidential positions about the person of the monarch.

It was natural that, so far away from their native land, these would-be Mexican rulers, stranded among a people with whose customs and mode of thought they had no sympathy, and of whose traditions they knew nothing, should cling to the little circle of trusted friends who had followed them in their adventure. It was natural also that the Mexicans, seduced by the vision of a monarchy in which THEY hoped to be the ruling force by virtue of their share in its inception and its establishment, should feel a keen disappointment upon finding foreigners, whom they themselves had been instrumental in placing at the head of affairs, not only overshadowing them, but usurping what they deemed their legitimate influence. It was likewise natural that the French, who had put up all the stakes for the game, and who had sacrificed lives, millions, and prestige in the venture, should look to a preponderant weight in the councils of an empire which was entirely of their creating. All this was the inevitable consequence of such a combination as that attempted in Mexico; but apparently it was one which had entered into no one's calculations, and for which no provision had been made. The imperial dream of Napoleon III had been too shadowy to include such humanities.

The original "king-makers" soon became a troublesome element in Maximilian's administration. His policy naturally led him to seek supporters among the progressive Mexicans, and to devise the honorable retirement of his early allies from the active management of affairs.

General Almonte from the first was set aside with empty honors.* In 1866 he was appointed to replace Senor Hidalgo as representative of Mexico to France. General Miramon and General Marquez were likewise sent away in honorable exile; and by degrees the more conspicuous among the reactionary leaders were put out of the way.

* He was made great marshal of the court, minister of the imperial household, and high chancellor of the imperial orders.

In March, 1864, Maximilian, about to sail from Miramar, had addressed a letter to President Juarez. In this curious document he spoke of himself as "the chosen of the people," and invited him to attach himself to the empire. He even offered him a distinguished place in its administration. This, of course, was haughtily declined by the President. But persevering efforts were made to win over, by promises of preferment, the leading men of the Liberal party. Some declined in noble terms, but others succumbed to the temptation, and for a while a decided tendency was shown to rally around the new order of things. Yet these conditions, favorable as they were, added to the complications of the situation. In a very short time, what with the difficulties arising from the nationalized clergy property, and with the personal disappointment of many of those who had made the empire, Maximilian found the men upon whose invitation he had come to Mexico turning away from him. Moreover, the influence of M. Eloin's policy had inaugurated the long series of misunderstandings between the court and the French quartier-general, which ultimately led to complications at first by no means unavoidable. "Non es emperador, es empeorador," was the pun popularly repeated by Mexican wags.* Six months had not elapsed since the regent Almonte had turned over to the young Emperor the quasi-consolidated empire conquered by Marshal Bazaine, and thinking men already foresaw the end. Never did the tide of success turn so rapidly.

* "Ce n'est pas un empereur; c'est un empireur." Compare Masaeras, "Un Essai d'Empire au Mexique," p. 42 (Paris, 1879).

In October, 1864, Comte de Thun de Hohenstein had been sent to Paris to negotiate for the transportation of some four thousand Austrians for the army of Maximilian in Mexico. Belgians were also rapidly enlisting under Colonel Van der Smissen; and shortly afterward Austro-Belgian auxiliary troops, numbering, from first to last, some eight thousand men, were transferred to Mexico.* These soon developed into an additional source of difficulty.

* See Galignani, October 14, 1864.

The officers of the Austrian contingent had not forgotten the yet recent encounters with the French army at Solferino and Magenta, and, no doubt at first unconsciously, an unconciliatory spirit was manifested in every difference which arose between the French and their present allies.

Comte de Thun, the commander of the Austrian corps, felt more than restless under Marshal Bazaine's authority. Eventually, in 1865, Maximilian, whose confidence he enjoyed, further complicated the situation by establishing alongside of the War Department a military cabinet, through which the Austro-Belgian contingents were independently administered. This broke up all chance of uniform action in military matters. It placed the auxiliary troops beyond the jurisdiction of the French commander, who, under the terms of the treaty of Miramar, was to be regarded as the commander-in-chief.

The same lack of unity that existed between the imperial army and the French was also found to exist between the foreign mercenaries and the Mexican troops.

To the natives these foreigners, although countrymen of their sovereigns, were interlopers and rivals. Their very presence defeated the object of their Emperor's futile attempt at a show of Mexican patriotism. The position of the French was a well-defined one. They were there for a purpose, spent their money freely, fought their battles victoriously, and would some day go back to France. But the Mexicans hated these foreigners, and the confidential offices held by impecunious Belgians and Austrians in the government and about the person of the chief executive added to the instinctive suspicion with which their permanent residence in the country was regarded.

Under the then existing conditions, where so many irreconcilable interests were in presence, it is not to be wondered at if little harmony prevailed amid the various conflicting elements gathered together by fate for the enactment of this fantastic scene.

The attitude of the United States toward the empire had been unmistakably emphasized on May 3, 1864, by the departure of our minister, the Hon. Thomas Corwin, who left, ostensibly on leave of absence, as soon as the approach of the new sovereigns was heralded.

His was an interesting personality. Tall, stout, and somewhat awkward in his gait, his double chin was lost between the exaggerated points of the stiff white collar so characteristic of our American statesmen at that time. His kindly smile and natural charm of voice and manner, however, soon attracted and held those who at first found him unengaging. With all his attainments he had preserved unspoiled a certain natural modesty, which led him to attribute his advancement to accident or fate. He once told me that he owed all his success in life to the fact that, as a country boy in Ohio, while driving his father's cart downhill at daybreak, he fell asleep and was jolted off his seat, breaking his leg. During the weeks of enforced seclusion that followed he taught himself to read, and developed a studious turn of mind, which, his leg having been permanently weakened by the accident, led him to seek a situation in a lawyer's office. From these humble beginnings he rose to the place he then occupied as one of our foremost orators and, since 1861, as minister to Mexico,* so that, he merrily added, he owed his fortune to a broken leg. Such men, however, are in no need of accidents to rise; Mr. Corvin could not help doing so from the innate buoyancy of his brilliant personality.

* He now left American affairs in the charge of his secretary of legation, his son William Corwin.

On April 4 the Senate and House of Representatives at Washington had passed a unanimous resolution in opposition to the recognition of a monarchy in Mexico, as an expression of the sentiment of the people of the United States. Secretary Seward, in forwarding a copy of the resolution to Mr. Dayton, our minister to France, had, however, instructed him to inform the French government that "the President does not at present contemplate any departure from the policy which this government has hitherto pursued in regard to the war which exists between France and Mexico."*

* See "Diplomatic Correspondence," 1865, Part III, p. 357.

Notwithstanding the small encouragement which such an attitude gave him, one of the earliest acts of Maximilian was to send Senor Arroyo to seek an interview with the head of the United States government, with a view to the recognition of the empire. Senor Arroyo was not even granted an audience. In July, 1865, another attempt was made by Maximilian with the same object in view.

Among the chamberlains of the Emperor at that time was a son of General Degollado, a Liberal leader who had been killed at Las Cruces, while fighting for the republic against General Marquez in 1861. Young Degollado had lived in Washington, and there had married an American woman. His attainments were mediocre and his personality was colorless, but his wife was ambitious and energetic. She was eager to see her husband come to the front, and, setting aside family traditions, did her best to encourage the imperial court in the idea that the United States government, if properly approached, might be brought to consider the recognition of the empire. She was a good-looking, pleasant woman, who readily made friends, and the couple were put forward as likely to bring the undertaking to a favorable conclusion.

It had at first been suggested that an envoy extraordinary be sent in full official pomp to Washington. General Almonte had been spoken of for the mission, and Mr. and Mrs. Degollado were to have accompanied him as members of the embassy. Senor Ramirez, the minister of state and a moderate Liberal of high standing and ability, realized, however, that the imperial government, in following such a course, must publicly expose itself to a slight. He therefore urged upon Maximilian a modification of the plan, and it was arranged that Mr. and Mrs. Degollado should go in a semi-official manner to prepare the ground and to feel the way.

Mrs. Degollado was much excited over the prospect, and even seemed sanguine of success. It was hinted that Mr. Corwin, then in Washington, was lending himself to certain intrigues designed to facilitate the negotiations.

The Emperor's agents arrived in Washington on July 17, 1865. M. de Montholon, who since 1864 had been minister of France to Mexico, endeavored to obtain an audience for "the chamberlain of Maximilian" as bearer of a letter from the Emperor of Mexico to the President.* But the mission proved a failure, and only added one more to the many abortive attempts made during those four years to "solve the unsolvable problem."**

* "Diplomatic Correspondence," 1865, Part III, p. 484.

** According to Prince Salm-Salm, yet another attempt was planned in the fall of 1866, in which he and his wife were intended to be the principal actors, and were to be sent to Washington armed with a fund of $2,000,000 in gold. He states that the news of the Empress's illness, and the consequent failure of her mission abroad, prevented the carrying out of the scheme.

On January 1, 1865, President Juarez issued from Chihuahua a proclamation in which he confessed defeat, but in dignified tones asserted the righteousness of the national cause, in which he put his trust, and appealed to the nobler ideals of his countrymen.

At that moment, to the superficial observer, and in the capital, the empire seemed an accomplished fact. The country at large, although by no means pacified, was nominally under imperial rule. Almost alone, in the south, General Porfirio Diaz held his own at Oajaca, and remained unsubdued.

General Courtois d'Hurbal, who had been sent against him, had so far been unable to deal with him. The commander-in-chief resolved once more to take the field in person. As a result, Oajaca shortly afterward was taken, and General Diaz, at last forced to surrender, was made prisoner, and transferred to Puebla for safe-keeping.*

* He, however, boldly managed his escape a few months later, and again took the field at the head of a band of fourteen men. These increased in number, snowball fashion, as other guerrillas gradually rallied around the distinguished chief; and, at the head of an army, he reappeared in Oajaca. After defeating

the famous decree of October 3, now known in Mexican history as the Bando Negro ("black decree"). In this fatal enactment he assumed that the war was at an end, and, while doing homage to President Juarez himself, attempted to brand all armed republicans as outlaws who, if taken in arms, must henceforth be summarily dealt with by the courts martial, or—when made prisoners in battle—by the military leader, and shot within twenty-four hours.*

* See Appendix A.

This extraordinary decree was greeted with dismay in the United States. It outraged the Mexicans, and excited the vindictiveness of the Liberal party. At the time such men as General Riva-Palacio and General Diaz were still in the field, and some of Mexico's most illustrious patriots were thus placed under a ban by the foreign monarch.*

* General Diaz's record is well-known and requires no comment here. General Riva-Palacio was a patriot and a gentleman. He was a man of parts, and had achieved some reputation as a poet and dramatic author. At the outbreak of the war he organized and equipped at his own expense a regiment, and was with General Zaragoza at Puebla. His division was one of the finest in the Mexican service, and, throughout the war, he loyally conducted his military operations in strict accordance with recognized usage. He cared for the wounded, exchanged prisoners, and, at the last, even went so far as to extend his protection to small detachments of French troops making their way to the Atlantic coast from the shores of the Pacific. See note from Marshal Bazaine, quoted in a letter from Mr. Bigelow to Mr. Seward, February 12, 1866 ("Diplomatic Correspondence," 1866, Part I, p. 281).

It has been claimed that Marshal Bazaine entered an earnest protest against the measure, the harshness of which he regarded as impolitic; that he urged its inexpediency, and personally objected to it as likely to weaken the authority of the military courts; that he, moreover, observed that it opened an avenue to private revenge, and delivered up the prisoners of one faction into the hands of another, a course which could not fail to add renewed bitterness to the civil war now so nearly at an end.* But although the famous decree certainly was the spontaneous act of the Emperor, and of his ministers who signed it, there can be no doubt that it embodied the policy of repression urged by the marshal, and that, if he cannot be held responsible for its form, in substance it "was approved by him.** "Whatever may have been its origin, when, shortly afterward (October 13, 1865), Generals Arteaga and Salazar, with others*** who, at the head of small detachments, were holding the country in the north against General Mendez, were taken by the latter, and shot, under the decree of October 3, such a clamor of indignation was raised at home and abroad as must have demonstrated his mistake to the young Emperor. This mistake he was soon to expiate with his own blood.

* See M. de Keratry, loc. cit., p. 84 et seq. See also debate in Chamber of Deputies, "Moniteur Universel" (Paris), Jan. 28,1866.

** See Louet, "La Verite sur l'Expedition du Mexique," etc., Part ii, "L'Empire de Maximilien," by P. Gaulot; also Prince Salm-Salm's "My Diary in Mexico," etc., in which the author states that he was told by Maximilian that the decree was drafted and amended by Marshal Bazaine, who urged its enactment. In the memorandum drawn up for his lawyers, and published by Dr. Basch in "Erinnerungen aus Mexico," Maximilian, says: "Bazaine dictated himself the details before witnesses."

*** Colonels Villagomez, Diaz Paracho, and Pedro Mina were among those who were shot. General Mendez was one of the best and most brilliant officers in the imperial army, and it may be said in extenuation of his personal share in the tragedy that the cruelty of the mode of warfare carried on by Arteaga and his lieutenants seemed to warrant stern treatment. It is stated that only a short time before Arteaga had caused the father of Mendez to be shot, and that but six weeks prior to his own capture, the commander of the garrison of Uruapan, Colonel Lemus, an old man of sixty-eight, and the prefect, D. Paz Gutierrez, had been put to death by his orders without judgment, or even time to write to their families (Domenech, loc. cit., vol. iii, p. 335).

PART IV.

THE AWAKENING

I. "A CLOUD NO BIGGER THAN A MAN'S HAND"

On March 10,1865, the Duc de Morny died. He had been the moving spirit in the Mexican imbroglio, and it would be difficult to believe that the withdrawal of the prompter did not have a weakening effect upon the performance. His death, by removing one of the strongest influences in favor of the intervention, not only in the Corps Legislatif and at court, but in the financial world, was certainly one of the many untoward circumstances which helped to hasten the end.

In France, the elections of 1863 and 1864 had added strength to the opposition. It now insisted upon being heard. Not only had the discussions of the budget in the Chamber of Deputies brought out with painful clearness the weight of the burden assumed by France, but private letters written by intelligent officers were gradually enlightening public opinion upon the true condition of affairs in Mexico. Some of these letters had even found their way to the Tuileries.

Public feeling was beginning to express in uncompromising tones the conviction that the government must relinquish an onerous task, the impossibility of accomplishing which was becoming patent. It was even openly suggested that the Tuileries must combine with "Washington for the purpose of establishing in Mexico a form of government acceptable to the latter".*

* See "Revue des Deux Mondes," 1865, vol. lviii, p. 776; also vol. lvii, pp. 768, 1018.

The writer of M. de Moray's obituary notice in the "Revue des Deux Mondes"* boldly asked whether the duke, who was always fortunate, and to whom success had become a habit, had not died opportunely. He left the question for the future to decide. The answer was not long delayed.**

* Ibid., 1865, vol. lvi, p. 501.

** And yet M. Rouher, in April, 1865, speaking for the French government in the Corps Legislatif, still affirmed that "France would continue to protect Mexico until the full consolidation of its undertaking" (ibid, vol. lvi, p. 1065).

The inauguration of the Mexican empire had been officially announced to the chambers by the government in the following terms: "The results obtained in 1862 and 1863 by our Corps Expeditionnaire in Mexico have, in 1864, received a solemn consecration under the protection of the flag of

France. A regular government has been founded in that country, heretofore for more than fifty years delivered up to anarchy and intestine dissensions. In the beginning of the month of June the Emperor Maximilian took possession of the throne, and, sustained by our army, he inaugurated in all security an era of peace and prosperity for his new country."

Jules Favre pertinently asked: "Since Maximilian is established; since Maximilian is the Messiah announced in all time past; since he is really the man both for the Indians and the Spaniards, who receive him with acclamation; since he meets on his passage only with bouquets from the senoritas—let our soldiers return. What have they to do in Mexico! They are not needed, and can only be an obstacle in the way of that entire unanimity of feeling that exists between the prince and the nation." He stated that rumors were reaching France of fierce battles, of martial law, of prisoners of war shot, of villages burned, holding up as an example San Sebastian, in Sinaloa, a town of four thousand souls, which had been entirely burned and destroyed by General Castagny during his campaign against Romero and in the name of Emperor Maximilian,* and then he proceeded to show the ghastly farce that had been enacted behind these words, in the light cast upon it by the blaze of the ill-fated town; "Why this discrepancy between the official statements as to the pacification of Mexico, the unanimous consent to Maximilian's elevation to the throne, and the facts, i.e., the country under martial law, and the French army, marching, torch in hand, protecting one party and punishing the other by the wholesale destruction of life and property? Why did such contradiction exist between the official statements as to universal suffrage, the freedom of the press, the unanimity of sentiment in Mexico, and the fact that journalists were being brought, in the name of the Emperor, before a council of war and condemned to various penalties for having expressed their criticism of such wholesale executions?"

* "Mexicans! I have come in the name of the Emperor Maximilian into the state of Sinaloa, to establish peace therein, to protect property, and to deliver you from the malefactors who oppress you under the mask of liberty," said General Castagny in his proclamation.

He resumed by calling attention to the renewed postponement of the ministry's promises with regard to the withdrawal of the army, and to its broken pledge that it would retire when Maximilian's throne was established and a proper impetus had been given to the work of regeneration. For the accomplishment of these ends, said the orator, a sacrifice of forty thousand men and a yearly expenditure of four or five millions would be needed for ten years to come.

In words which now sound prophetic he eloquently referred to Napoleon I and to his Spanish campaign, likewise undertaken under the pretense of regenerating a nation. "The mighty man who had conceived such projects," he cried, "all know where they led him. On April 14, 1814, the sentence of deposition thus expressed the motives of the Senate for deposing him: 'WHEREAS, Napoleon Bonaparte has undertaken a series of wars in violation of Article L of the Constitution of the 22d Frimaire, year 8, which provides that declarations of war must be proposed, discussed, and promulgated like laws; WHEREAS, The liberty of the press, established and consecrated as one of the rights of nations, has been constantly subject to the arbitrary 164 censorship of the police,'" etc., and as he closed his argument he said:

"After a thorough study of all the facts in the case, political, military, and financial, it is impossible for any one seriously to believe that the government of Maximilian can exist without our army. With our army, I acknowledge it, his throne would rest upon an agreement, it would last as long as our assistance should be extended to it, but if you withdraw this assistance it is evident that it will be overthrown. If, therefore, you wish to establish it firmly, our army must remain in Mexico: the Chamber should understand this thoroughly."

Only thirteen members of the Chamber voted against the appropriation for the maintenance of the Corps Expeditionnaire; but it has been pointed out, and it is only fair to believe, that many voted for it who, as Frenchmen, felt that the government, blameworthy as it might be, should not be compelled suddenly to abandon an adventure in which the honor of France was involved. French patience, however, was fast nearing its limit, and when, in 1864, Maximilian accepted the crown, he must have realized that French support could not be indefinitely counted upon.

The millions raised through the Mexican loans had been carelessly administered and lavishly spent. What with the expenses of the court, extensive alterations in the imperial residences, especially in Chapultepec, and the outlay incidental to the pageants and ovations of the Emperor's journeys in the provinces, the relief brought by the loans had been brief.

Confidence was waning. The incapacity of Maximilian was becoming generally recognized, and the difficulties inherent in the situation were everywhere growing clearer.

Maximilian had alienated Borne, whose censure he had drawn upon himself by his effort to conciliate the moderate party. He had aroused the resentment of the priests and brought upon himself the remonstrances of the bishops, and had set aside, or sent to foreign posts, the leaders of the party to whom he owed his crown. Yet he had not succeeded in winning over from the Liberal party any very important adhesions to his government.

Cardinal Antonelli, in a letter dated December 27, 1864, after setting forth the grievances of the holy see, stated that the Holy Father hoped that Maximilian in abandoning the course marked out in his letter to the minister, Senor Escudero, would "spare the holy see the necessity of taking proper measures to set right in the eyes of the world the responsibility of the august chief of the church—measures of which the least, certainly, would not be the recall of the pontifical representative in Mexico, in order that he may not remain there a powerless spectator of the spoliation of the church and of the violation of its most sacred rights."*

* "Diplomatic Correspondence," 1865, Part III, p. 623.

It is difficult to understand why Maximilian had not negotiated the terms of a concordat with the holy see when he went to Rome to receive the Pope's blessing before leaving Europe for his new dominions. The adjustment of existing differences between church and state formed the most urgent as well as the most vital issue to be met by the young Emperor, as upon the settlement of the vexed question of ownership in clergy property must depend the restoration of business confidence and of prosperity in the empire. The pretensions advanced by the papal nuncio sent by the Vatican to arrange for a concordat now proved so exorbitant that Maximilian had been compelled to decline to consider them, and he and the holy see had failed to come to terms. The final and official rupture with Monsignor Meglia took place in December, 1864. It was made public in a decree issued by Maximilian which proclaimed that papal bulls should not receive exequatur until approved by the chief executive.

The fact was that the party through which the French and Maximilian had been called to Mexico was the unpopular retroactive party; that, in order to exist, Maximilian had been obliged to recognize the measures enacted against his own partizans by the national party; that in so doing he had disappointed the priests; that in setting aside the leaders of the clerical party he had estranged his strongest adherents; and all this without making any serious headway with his antagonists, who would have no emperor, no monarchy, no foreigner.

The success of the intervention was now clearly seen to depend upon a war systematically conducted against an enemy that represented a national sentiment.

On January 23, 1865, the governments of Chili, Bolivia, Salvador, Colombia, Peru, and Venezuela formed a defensive alliance against exterior aggression and for the guaranty of their respective autonomy. The treaty was signed in Lima by the representatives of the nations interested.

But a far more serious danger was threatening the empire in the North. On April 9, 1865, General Lee surrendered to the Federal army. The Civil War in the United States was at an end, and the French were beginning to understand that the Northern republic, whose unbroken unity stood strengthened, could no longer remain a passive spectator of the struggle taking place at its frontier.

The scene of military interest suddenly shifted to the Rio Grande, and the incidents happening on the border deserved more attention than Maximilian seemed at first inclined to bestow.

The interests of the national party were represented in Washington by Senor Romero, who, with consummate tact and ability, made the most of every opportunity. The service rendered by him to the cause of republicanism and of Mexican independence was second to none in importance. No detail seemed too trifling to be turned to account in his effort to strengthen the Mexican cause with our government.

A rumor reached us that President Juarez had succeeded in raising a loan in the United States. The ranks of the Liberal army were receiving important reinforcements from the officers and men of General Banks's command, who passed the border in large numbers to take part in the attack of General Cortinas at Matamoros. Already, in January, 1865, the impulse given to the Republican party in the North vibrated throughout the land. Soon resistance everywhere appeared in arms once more. Both General Mejia and Admiral Cloue, then in command of the French Gulf Squadron, complained that the United States army afforded protection to the Juarists.

Recruiting-offices had been opened in New York, which, although not countenanced by the government, must have furnished valuable auxiliaries to the Liberals. Alarming rumors reached France and Mexico with regard to the extent of the movement.

On the other hand, the negotiations then being carried on between Napoleon and Maximilian, with a view to securing the Mexican debt to France by a lien upon the mines of Sonora, were causing uneasiness in the United States, and gave rise to considerable diplomatic correspondence.*

* See, in this connection, "Diplomatic Correspondence," 1865, Part III, pp. 357-363, 417, and letter of Secretary Seward addressed to Mr. Bigelow, February 17, 1865.

It required no wizard to foretell the issue. After the surrender of General Lee, a Confederate army-corps, twenty-five thousand strong, acting through General Slaughter, had opened negotiations with Marshal Bazaine, with a view to passing the border and settling in northern Mexico, provided suitable terms were granted by the Mexican government to the new colonists. It was then becoming clear to many that the halfway policy hitherto followed had led to nothing, and must result in a useless sacrifice of life and millions unless a larger force were maintained by the French in Mexico, or some barrier set up against the naturally dominant position taken by the United States with regard to Mexican affairs.

In June, 1865, Generals Kirby Smith, Magruder, Shelby, Slaughter, Walker, A. W. Terrell of Texas, Governor Price of Missouri, General Wilcox of Tennessee, Commodore Maury of Virginia, General Hindman of Arkansas, Governor Reynolds of Georgia, Judge Perkins, Colonel Denis, and Mr. Pierre Soule of Louisiana, Major Mordecai of North Carolina, and others, had come to Mexico. With them had passed over the frontier horses, artillery, everything that could be transported, including large and small bands of Confederate soldiers, and some two thousand citizens who left the United States with the intention of colonizing Sonora.

Confederate officers now flocked to Mexico with a view to making new homes for themselves. Many of them were interested in special schemes by which the agricultural wealth of the land might be made to yield its treasure to the ruined but experienced Southern planters.

My mother being a Southern woman, and knowing some of their leaders, our house soon became a center where they gathered in the evening and freely discussed their hopes. Thus was added a new element to the already motley assemblage which collected about us at that time. Truly a most heterogeneous set! Confederate officers, members of the diplomatic corps, newly fledged chamberlains and officials of the palace, the marshal's officers,—Frenchmen, Austrians, Belgians, and a few Mexicans,—would drop in, each group bringing its own interests, and, alas! its animosities.

Laws against foreigners having been passed, no property could henceforth be held by them unless they became naturalized. Some of the Confederate refugees therefore became Mexican citizens, and took service under the Mexican government. Governor Price, for instance, received authorization to recruit the imperial army in the Confederacy. He and Governor Harris of Tennessee and Judge Perkins of Louisiana were appointed agents of colonization, and immediately set to work upon the survey of the region lying between Mexico and Vera Cruz, with a view to furthering this purpose. General Magruder, the ex-commander-in-chief of the Confederate forces in Texas, having also become naturalized, was placed in charge of the survey of the lands set aside for colonization as chief of the Colonization Land Office. The government sold such land to colonists for the nominal consideration of one dollar an acre, and allowed every head of a family to purchase six hundred and forty acres upon a credit of five years. A single man was allowed three hundred and twenty acres.

Not only the government, but large landowners, proposed such free grants, and offered every inducement to settlers, if they would come and develop the agricultural resources of the country. The first Confederate settlement was established near Cordoba in the autumn of 1865.

Commodore Maury, now a naturalized Mexican citizen, had in September been appointed imperial commissioner of immigration and councilor of state. He opened an office in the Calle San Juan de Lateran, and was authorized to establish agencies in the Southern States.* But the indecision and weakness of Maximilian prevented his taking full advantage of the opportunity then offered to strengthen the empire. The delay caused by a vacillating policy discouraged the would-be colonists, and before long the flood of immigration was checked.

* See decrees signed by Maximilian and the minister of the interior, D. Luis Robles Pezuela, on September 24 and 27.

General Charles P. Stone had come to Mexico with a colonization scheme of his own. He had, in 1859, made a survey of Sonora under the Jecker contract. He now was on his way to look after some of the Jecker claims when accident threw him on board of the steamer with Dr. William M. Gwin, ex-senator for California. The two men at once came to an understanding and joined forces.

In 1856 (December 19), two years after the filibustering expedition of Count Raousset de Boulbon, the house of Jecker had obtained from the Mexican government the right to survey the territories of Sonora and southern California. The conditions were that one third of the unclaimed land should become the property of the house of Jecker.

In 1859 the Liberal government had rescinded the grant, and this had added one more grievance to those which the Swiss banker had brought up against the administration of Juarez. No sooner had Sonora sent in its adhesion to the empire than Jecker proposed to the French government to make over his rights against a payment of two million dollars.

The plan was then to colonize Sonora and Lower California, establishing, on behalf of France, a right to exploit the mines. The climate was healthful, the land rich, the adventure tempting; but it had the great drawback of running foul of the most acute Mexican susceptibilities. Not only did such pretensions at that time excite the suspicions of the Mexicans with regard to the disinterestedness of the French alliance, but they were calculated to give umbrage to the United States government.

As early as 1863, Napoleon III had discussed the possibility of establishing in Sonora* a colony which should develop the mining and agricultural wealth of the state. In exchange for a grant of unclaimed national lands, these colonists were to pay a percentage of their proceeds to France, as well as a tax to the Mexican government.

* Chihuahua, Durango, and Sinaloa eventually were also included in the scheme.

A colony of armed Confederates, inimical to the Federal government of the United States, established between its dominions and the heart of the Mexican empire, and backed by France, Austria, and Belgium, must form a formidable bulwark in case of trouble between Mexico and its Northern neighbor. There is small doubt that some such plan had formed a part of the original "deal" proposed by Jecker to the French leaders.

In the spring of 1864 unauthorized attempts had been made by Californian immigrants to land at Guaymas and settle upon certain lands granted them by President Juarez. The marshal had sent French troops to protect the province from such inroads, treating these intruders as squatters. This had furnished a reason for the military occupation of Sonora; thus was the first step taken in the realization of the project.

Such was, in rough outline, the position of the Sonora colonization question when Dr. Gwin entered upon the scene. Upon his arrival in Mexico, he applied at headquarters for an audience. The marshal, although in full sympathy with the project, realized the danger of its open discussion at that time. Maximilian and his advisers were opposed to it. Much tact and secrecy seemed, therefore, necessary in the conduct of negotiations having for their object the furtherance of so unpopular a scheme. Dr. Gwin was too conspicuous a figure to pass unnoticed the portals of the French headquarters. An informal interview was therefore arranged.

We then lived at Tacubaya, a suburb of Mexico reached by the Paseo, where the marshal rode every day for exercise. Our house was built at the foot of a long hill, at the top of which stood a large old mansion, the yellow coloring of which had won for it the name of the Casa Amarilla. It had been rented by Colonel Talcott of Virginia, who lived there with his family. Dr. Gwin was their guest; and it was arranged that the marshal, when taking his usual afternoon ride with his aide-de-camp, should call upon us one day, and leaving the horses in our patio with his orderlies, should join us in a walk up the hill, casually dropping in en passant at the Casa Amarilla.

The plan had the double advantage of being a simple one and of providing the marshal, who did not speak English, with suitable interpreters. The interview was a long one. The marshal listened to what the American had to say. Indeed, there was little to be said on his own side, as the Mexican ministry was absolutely opposed to the project, and any change of policy must depend upon a change in the imperial cabinet.

His Excellency, however, seemed in high good humor. As we came out, he merrily challenged us to run downhill, much to the astonishment of the few leperos whom we happened to meet. The Mexican Indian is a sober, rather somber creature, not given to levity; his amusements are of a dignified, almost sad nature. He may be sentimental, bigoted, vicious, cruel, but he is never vulgar, and is seldom foolish. Indeed, well might they stare at us then, for it was no common sight in the lanes of Tacubaya to see a commander-in-chief tearing downhill, amid peals of laughter, with a party of young people, in utter disregard of age, corpulence, and cumbersome military accoutrements!

The personality of Dr. Gwin was a strong one. A tall, broad, squarely built man, with rough features which seemed hewn out of a block with an ax, ruddy skin, and a wealth of white hair brushed back from his brow, all combined to make him by far the most striking figure among the group of Southern leaders then assembled in Mexico.

His own faith in the almightiness of his will influenced others, and in this case brought him very near to success. He talked willingly and fluently of his plans. Notwithstanding the decided opposition met with on the part of the Mexican government, he then confidently expected to be installed in the new colony by the opening of the year, and invited his friends to eat their Christmas dinner with him there. He was generous in sharing his prospects with them. We all were to be taken in and made wealthy: every dollar invested was to return thousands, every thousand, millions!

It was entertaining to hear him narrate his interviews at the Tuileries with Napoleon III and the other great men of the day. His tone was that of a potentate treating with his peers. He spoke of "my policy," "my colony," "my army," etc.

In 1865 Dr. Gwin again went to Prance to confer with its ruler. Upon his return to Mexico, he was regarded as the unofficial agent of the French government. The Emperor had promised him every facility and assistance. All that was now needed to make his dreams a brilliant reality was the signature of Maximilian. He was full of glowing anticipations. But Maximilian, who at the time was none too friendly to his allies, stood firm.* However much the French might urge it, the national feeling was already strongly arrayed against any plan involving the possible alienation of any part of the Mexican territory. Moreover, it was becoming obvious, from the various complications occurring upon the Rio Grande, that the befriending of the Confederate refugees must henceforth seriously add to the difficulty of obtaining the recognition of the Mexican empire by the United States—an end which Maximilian had greatly at heart, and one which, strangely enough, he never lost the hope of accomplishing, so little did he, even after two years' residence in Mexico, understand American conditions.

* Later he laid stress upon his attitude with regard to this. In the memorandum written by him for the use of his lawyers at his trial in vindication of his conduct, he urged as a claim to Mexican leniency his firm resistance to French pretensions concerning the disposal of Sonora, and his loyal effort to maintain the integrity of the Mexican territory, and declared that this drew upon him the hostility of the French. See S. Basch, "Erinnerungen aus Mexico." (This interesting document is not given in the French edition.)

On June 26, 1865, Marshal Bazaine was married to Mlle. de la Pena. The Emperor and Empress expressed a wish that the ceremony and wedding breakfast should take place at the imperial palace. No effort was spared by them to make the occasion a memorable one: Empress Charlotte bestowed upon the bride a set of diamonds; the Emperor gave her as a dowry the palace of San Cosme, a noble residence, valued at one hundred thousand dollars, where the French had established their headquarters since the beginning of the intervention. Every one was in good humor, many polite assurances of appreciation and good will were exchanged on both sides, and for a while it seemed as though harmony might be restored among the leaders. But this pleasant state of affairs was of short duration. The difficulties inherent in the situation were too conspicuous, and the causes of ill feeling were too deeply laid, to be overcome by other than superior men. Notwithstanding a superficial improvement in Mexican conditions, it was becoming patent in the summer of 1865 that nothing short of a miracle could save all concerned from disaster and humiliation.

In those days, our social circle varied from year to year according to the political and military conditions of the hour. Occasionally the arrival of some distinguished newcomer on a special mission from abroad would create a stir among us.

The advent, toward the close of the year 1865, of M. Langlais, the fifth financier sent by Napoleon III to organize the finances of the empire, caused considerable excitement and aroused the hopes of the court. His appointment to succeed M. de Bonnefons had been heralded by the French official papers with much pomposity.

He came ostensibly to act as minister of finance (without a portfolio), at an enormous salary, and was supposed, by those who sent him, to take the full direction of Mexican financial affairs.

He was a councilor of state, and was possessed large experience of French politics. A ministerial official, methodical, precise, fresh from the well-appointed offices of the French government, he arrived at Vera Cruz just as a guerrilla band, after taking up the rails of the only railway then laid upon Mexican soil, had attacked a train and massacred its escort of French soldiers.

The poor man's stereotyped ideas of existence were considerably shaken up by the occurrence; but he was a firm believer in his own capacity, and was disposed to attribute the failures of his predecessors to their inferiority to himself. He won the confidence and personal regard of the young sovereigns, and unhesitatingly undertook to raise the public revenue, then of eighty-four millions of dollars, to one hundred and twenty millions. How far he might have gone toward fulfilling his promise it is impossible to tell, for he died suddenly on February 23, 1866.*

* M. Langlais is stated to have said that he was working to give Maximilian the chance to abdicate honorably; but the favor in which he was held at court makes such a statement doubtful.

His death was a blow to the court, where he stood in high favor. The Empress Charlotte especially is said to have detected in it the finger of a fate adverse to the empire. This calamity was soon followed by another, well calculated to cast the gloom of a dark shadow across the path of the young princess.

Her father, King Leopold I, had died December 10, 1865. Upon his accession to the throne, her brother, King Leopold II, sent a special embassy to the court of Mexico to make an official announcement of his reign. The ambassador, General Foury, arrived with his suite on February 14, 1866, and, having fulfilled his mission, departed on March 4. During their brief visit to the capital, the Belgian envoys had been freely entertained by society. It was, therefore, with a thrill of horror that, on the day following their departure, the news came that their party had been attacked and fired upon by highwaymen at Rio Frio, a few leagues from the capital, and that Baron d'Huart, officier d'ordonnance of the Count of Flanders, had been shot in the head and killed. Four other members of the embassy were wounded. Consternation reigned at court. The Emperor went to Rio Frio to see personally to the comfort of the wounded and to bring back the body of Baron d'Huart, whose solemn obsequies were conducted in the most impressive manner.

The news of this tragedy, when it reached Europe, must have cast a flash of lurid light upon the true condition of the Mexican empire.

During the winter of 1866 Napoleon III sent Baron Saillard upon a special mission to prepare Maximilian for the gradual withdrawal of the French army, and to intimate to him that he must not depend upon a continuance of present conditions. The envoy, however, failed to make upon the prince the impression which it was intended that he should make. Maximilian received him only twice, and rather resented his warnings. His visit only added to the coldness of the young Emperor's relations with the French.

Shortly afterward General Almonte was sent to France on a mission, the object of which, was to influence Napoleon to continue his support. The only result of his errand was a communication addressed to Maximilian, dated May 31, 1866. In this Napoleon stated the situation with a frankness the brutality of which aroused the indignation of the court of Mexico. An onerous agreement was nevertheless arrived at, to which necessity compelled Maximilian to subscribe (July 30). By this agreement, half of the revenue derived from the customs of Tampico and Vera Cruz was to be assigned to the French in payment of the debt until the entire outlay made on behalf of the Mexican empire had been repaid. The French, in return, promised to continue their support until November 1, 1867, and to withdraw their army in three detachments, the last of which would embark on that date. The imperial government was thereby deprived of half of its reliable revenue at a time when, in order to maintain its existence under the present stress, large additional resources should have been at its command.*

* See Appendix B.

The years 1865 and 1866 had been spent in administrative experiments. At first French officers detached from the service were placed in the various departments of the government as undersecretaries, in the hope of bringing about an honest and efficient organization without giving undue umbrage to the Mexicans. Members of the marshal's own household served thus in the War Department and in the Emperor's military office.

But the efforts of the French to introduce regularity into the various offices of the administration were so hampered that, even had the task been an easy one, it is not likely that much could have been accomplished. They had everything against them, even their allies and the monarch whom they wished to serve.

When, however, in 1866, the situation was found to be desperate, the Emperor, seriously alarmed, became more earnest and called the French to the rescue. Colonel Loysel was made chief of the military office of the Emperor, and the full control of the departments of War and of Finance was given respectively to Colonel Osmont, the chief of staff of the Corps Expeditionnaire, and to M. Friant, the chief of its commissariat.

But at this time there was not a dollar in the treasury; the sources of imperial revenue were daily diminishing; and the expenses of the government were now paid by the marshal out of the French treasury, under his own responsibility. The hour had been allowed to go by when organization was possible.

The marshal felt—and this feeling was shared by others—that neither Colonel Osmont nor M. Friant should have accepted a position of trust impossible to fill with credit at a time when France had resolved to withdraw its support from Maximilian. Their action was attributed to personal motives. The marshal declined to cooperate with or to help them, and they became an additional source of trouble. Later on, when, the Liberal cabinet having withdrawn, Maximilian once more turned to the reactionary party and called to power the clericals, he retained the above-mentioned Frenchmen in their departments. This affectation of confidence only added to the general ill feeling.

Under the conditions of open hostility then existing between the French and Mexican governments the interests of each were too wide apart for such a connection to continue without danger. A request from the commander-in-chief to MM. Osmont and Friant that they choose between their present ministerial functions and their respective positions in the Corps Expeditionnaire gave rise to a correspondence between the marshal and the Emperor, in the course of which the aggressive insistence of the latter compelled the former to refer the matter to the home government.

M. Drouyn de Lhuys upheld the marshal. And well it was that he did, for just then Mr. Seward, in a diplomatic note to M. de Montholon, under date of August 16, 1866,* peremptorily called his attention to the fact that the presence of the two French officers in the imperial cabinet was calculated to interfere with the good relations existing between France and the United States.

* "Diplomatic Correspondence," 1866, Part I, p. 381 et seq.

As a result of this communication, the marshal was censured by his government for not having at once prevented the above-mentioned officers from accepting their respective portfolios. The irritation on all sides was painfully visible.

II. LA DEBACLE

Matamoros had fallen in July, 1866. Now, while preparing for the difficult task of withdrawing his troops in the presence of an advancing army, the marshal sought not only to obey the instructions of the home government, but to serve the empire by concentrating its defense within possible limits and by placing between it and the northern frontier a natural barrier of wilderness in which "neither friend nor toe could easily subsist."*

* Letter of Bazaine to Maximilian, Peotillos, August 12, 1866.

The movement was not only planned in order to facilitate the country's defense against the Liberal forces, but also to guard against any possible aggression on the part of its formidable Northern neighbor after the withdrawal of the French army. This eminently prudent strategy was, however, irritating to Maximilian, who complained of it in the bitterest terms.

Article I of the preamble of the treaty of Miramar, signed in April, 1864, provided that "the French troops actually in Mexico shall, as soon as possible, be reduced to a corps of twenty-five thousand men, including the foreign legion." This corps was temporarily to remain in order to protect the interests in which the French intervention had been undertaken, but under the following conditions:

ARTICLE II. The French troops shall gradually evacuate Mexico as H. M. the Emperor of Mexico shall be able to organize the troops necessary to take their place.

ARTICLE III. The foreign legion in the service of France, composed of eight thousand men, shall, however, remain for six years in Mexico after all other French forces shall have been recalled under Article II. From that date said legion shall pass into the service and pay of the Mexican government, the Mexican government reserving unto itself the right to shorten the duration of the employment in Mexico of the foreign legion.

Permission had been granted to French officers to take service in this legion. Recruits were also expected from Europe, and twelve hundred Austrians, on the eve of embarking at St. Nazaire, were stopped only by the peremptory interference of the United States.* Various army-corps had been formed, officered by foreigners, among whom were some good French and Austrian officers. Much interest had at first been shown in the scheme; and the new army, its recruits, its uniforms and equipment, furnished society with a fruitful theme for conversation. For a time it had seemed as though it might be possible to so strengthen the empire as to enable it to stand without French official assistance. In 1866, however, Napoleon formally instructed the marshal to advance no more funds and to pay only the auxiliary troops. The Mexican army might dissolve. The French, on withdrawing, would leave the Austro-Belgian corps and the foreign legion,—i.e., some fifteen thousand men,—upon which the empire must depend. Under the new arrangement the Austro-Belgian soldiers were to receive the same pay as the French,—that is, about one half the amount formerly paid them,—and were once more placed under French control.**

* See "Diplomatic Correspondence," May, 1866, Part I, p. 305 et seq.

** Maximilian's proclamation to the auxiliary troops that they should henceforth form one and the same division "with their companions in arms" was dated May 19, 1866.

Dissatisfaction prevailed, and the very worst spirit was manifested on all sides. After continued ill feeling, in August, 1866, Comte de Thun sent in his resignation and returned to Europe, leaving Colonel Kodolitch in command.

The Belgian corps mutinied, and the ringleaders having been discharged, the disbanded men were incorporated into new mixed regiments.*

* Order given through General Neigre, July 8, 1866. The adjustment with the Austrians was no easier. An effort was made to induce the French to advance the pay for the auxiliary corps without proper accounts being submitted. To this, of course, they could not consent; and it was whispered that the affair resulted in the exposure of peculations on the part of certain individuals, whose resignation from the service General de Thun forthwith required. The better element of the Austrian army felt deeply humiliated by the incident, and it led to undisguised bitterness on all sides.

Meantime the Liberals were everywhere assuming an aggressive attitude. Guadalajara had fallen into the hands of General Uraga.

About this time an important convoy from Matamoros, under the escort of Colonel Olvera's Mexican force, sixteen hundred strong, and of an Austrian regiment, was attacked by Liberal forces. The officer in charge of the Austrian forces was then in the capital. The escort was overwhelmed, routed, and almost annihilated, and the convoy fell into the hands of the enemy. The Austrian officer had to bear the most severe and unsparing criticism from the French. The night after the news of the disaster had reached the capital he appeared at an evening gathering at the house of Countess de N—, the wife of an officer on the marshal's staff. As he entered, a perceptible shock was felt; electricity was in the air; many turned away from him, and an officer remarked in audible tones, as I asked the reason of the flutter: "O, ce n'est rien; c'est seulement le colonel, . . . qui aime mieux s'amuser a Mexico que de se battre a Matamoros."

It is more than likely that the officer, a man of proved courage, was fully justified by circumstances known to himself and to his chiefs in having left his post, but the spirit of antagonism then prevailing would admit of no excuse. The ill feeling existing between the Emperor and the marshal was fast spreading in every direction, and interfered even with the pleasure of social intercourse; and yet all this time the Emperor was writing to the marshal notes the tone of which was generally more than courteous, and signed himself "votre tres affectionne."

The fall of Matamoros marked the beginning of the end.

While reviewing the peripetia of an episode in which ignoble intrigue and treachery have so large a share, it is restful for a moment to pause before the modest figure of General Mejia, whose loyalty was unflinching to the bitter end. The brave Indian had for many months faithfully defended this important post. As true to his flag as President Juarez was to his, he himself had supplied the needs of his army, holding his own and never murmuring until, almost forgotten by his government, he was allowed to fall.

In July, 1866, Tampico and Monterey were, like Matamoros, lost to the Imperialists. The revenue derived from the port of Tampico thereby ceased altogether, and went to strengthen the national party. This event caused a painful shock.

To us in Mexico there was no concealing the fact that the knell of the Mexican empire had struck. Maximilian must fall. How? was the only question.

When, in the course of the winter, the treasury being empty, he had appealed to the French for relief, he had threatened to resign the throne unless they would advance to his administration the funds necessary for its support. The marshal had then, against the formal orders of his own government, supplied the millions necessary to tide over successive crises as they presented themselves; for it was clear that unless funds were immediately forthcoming the empire must collapse.

The French government, however, had censured the marshal's conduct. His situation was fast becoming an impossible one, and in order to obtain security for the French outlay he ordered the seizure of the custom-house of Vera Cruz. Maximilian was furious, and a rumor spread that he was seriously considering his abdication. The Empress, who strongly opposed his taking this step, suggested going abroad herself to see what could be done to save the crown. All confidence was at an end between the young monarchs and the marshal, whom they held responsible for Napoleon's altered attitude. It seemed to them idle to trust to written appeals the force of which must be counteracted by his representations. A personal interview might, however, accomplish much. The situation was reaching an acute crisis. Much bitter recrimination had followed upon the disasters to the imperial forces in the North. Nothing could be worse than the animus on both sides. Altogether, imperial Mexico had become a seething caldron, in which the scum stood a fair chance of rising to the top.

The imperial government, which during the first years of its existence had shown so much jealousy of its own authority, now suddenly changed its policy and sought to throw the whole weight of its responsibilities upon the French. In August, 1866, Maximilian proposed to face the uprising of the republicans throughout the empire, as well as to guard against possible aggression on the part of the United States troops then watching events across the Rio Grande, by declaring a state of siege throughout the empire and by placing the whole executive power of each state in the hands of a

French officer. This he urged upon the marshal, who courteously but firmly declined. It was impossible to tell where such a course, if adopted, would lead the French. It must necessarily carry with it serious consequences, the most obvious of which was a probable war with Mexico's Northern neighbor, and there is little doubt that this possibility prompted the suggestion.

Each side accused the other of duplicity with regard to the United States. The Imperialists openly charged the French with delivering up the empire to the republicans, while the French suspected the existence of snares and intrigues set afoot for the purpose of bringing about such complications as might force the French to retain an interest in Mexican affairs. Moreover, attempts, not wholly unsuccessful, were made to sow discord among the French themselves by taking advantage of individual ambitions and of petty jealousies to increase existing difficulties.

The relations between General Douay, then in command of the second division, and the quartier-general had never been cordial. On his way to France, on leave of absence, he passed through the city, and had an interview with Maximilian. This gave rise to much gossip. It was said that General Douay favored a policy totally different from that lately pursued by France, and that he approved of calling upon the French government for reinforcements for the purpose of firmly maintaining the empire; that he and Maximilian had arranged to bring pressure to bear upon the Emperor Napoleon not only to continue but to increase his support, and that Maximilian wished to see General Douay assume command of the French army in the marshal's place.

All this came to nothing, but the relations of the Emperor with the French headquarters were becoming more and more strained, and having begun with political differences, the feud was assuming almost a personal character.

Had Maximilian's grasp of the situation been stronger, he must have seen that by firmly taking his stand upon his original agreement with France, by refusing to consider the onerous terms substituted for those of the treaty of Miramar by Napoleon in his communication of May 31,1866, and by making then and there a public renunciation of his throne, based upon the non-fulfilment of the terms of the convention, he must throw the full responsibility of the denouement upon the Emperor of the French.*

* M. Rouher (July 10, 1866) announced to the Chamber of Deputies that the government had reluctantly determined upon the evacuation of Mexico by the army, owing to the inability of the Mexican government to observe the conditions of the treaty of Miramar. See Domenech, "Histoire," etc., vol. iii., p. 349.

He had then his one chance to retire with dignity and honor from the lamentable situation into which his youthful ambition and inexperience had led him, at the same time revenging himself upon his disloyal ally by exposing to the full light of day, and before the whole world, the wretched conditions under which the empire had been erected.

By compromising and signing away half the revenues of his ports,* by retaining the scepter upon terms that made the empire impossible, that forced him down to the level of a mere leader of faction, and placed him in contradiction to his own declared principles, he descended from his imperial state, and forfeited, if not his crown, at least his right to it, if judged by his own standard. He, moreover, lost his one chance of seriously embarrassing his allies. At that time the army was scattered in small detachments over the Mexican territory; terms had not yet been made with the Liberal leaders; the sudden collapse of the empire must have created dangers to the French, the existence of which would give him a certain hold over them.

* Convention of Mexico, signed July 30, 1866, by M. Dano and Don Luis de Arroyo.

But he was a weak man; the Empress clung to her crown; the great state officials were interested in retaining their offices; he was surrounded by evil or interested councilors; and instead of standing up firmly in his false ally's path, he allowed him to brush past and to disregard him.

In ancient Mexico, when, fortune having deserted a warrior, he fell into the hands of his enemies, a victim doomed to sacrifice, a chance was, under certain conditions, given him for his life. He was tied by one foot, naked, to the gladiatorial stone, armed with a wooden sword, and six warriors were, one after another, entered against him. If extraordinarily skilful, strong, and brave, he might hold his own and save his life; at least he might destroy some of his foes, and, falling like a warrior, avoid being laid alive upon the sacrificial stone, where his heart, torn out of his breast, must be held up, a bleeding sacrifice to the fierce god of battles.

Maximilian was not strong enough for the unequal struggle at this supreme moment, and he was laid upon the sacrificial stone.

Meanwhile the cloud "no bigger than a man's hand," which wise men had from the first anxiously watched as it loomed upon the northern horizon, had grown with alarming rapidity, and was now spreading black and threatening over the whole sky.

Secretary Seward was prepared to enter upon the scene. Nothing could be finer than the conduct of the American statesman throughout these difficult transactions. Alone among the foreign leaders who had a share in them, he followed a consistent policy from beginning to end, and his diplomatic notes form a logical sequence. Quietly, steadily, he played his part, to the greater credit and higher dignity of the nation whose interests and honor were in his keeping.

The burden of the Civil War had for several years weighed him down; but despite every effort of European diplomacy, the ship of state, steered by a firm hand, was kept upon its course, avoiding every shoal, while saving its strength for home defense. He never yielded a serious point, never wavered in his adherence to the traditional American policy, and stood by the legal republican government of Mexico even when, reduced to the persons of the President and his minister, Lerdo de Tejada, it was compelled to seek refuge at Paso del Norte. But when the surrender of Lee's army left the Federal government free to act, sixty thousand men were massed upon the frontier, and the American statesman at once grew threatening.*

* See peremptory note of Secretary Seward to Mr. Bigelow, November 23, 1866 ("Diplomatic Correspondence," 1866, Part I, p. 366). See also letter to the Marquis de Montholon, April 25, 1866.

In vain did Napoleon III plead for delay; in vain did he assure Mr. Bigelow that a date had been fixed for the final recall of the army. From Washington came the uncompromising words: No delay can be tolerated; the intervention and the empire must come to an end at once.*

* On December 10, 1860, Mr. Seward officially expressed his opinion that the traditional friendship with France would be brought into "imminent jeopardy, unless France could deem it consistent with her interest and honor to desist from the prosecution of armed intervention in Mexico" (letter of Seward to Bigelow, "Diplomatic Correspondence," 1866, Part III, p. 429); and he declined the condition made by the Emperor that the United States recognize the empire of Mexico as a de facto power. See proclamation of President Johnson, August 18, 1866, declaring the blockade of Matamoros issued by Maximilian null and void ("Diplomatic Correspondence," 1866, Part I, p. 339).

Since accepting Napoleon's ultimatum, by the terms of which all French assistance was to be withdrawn by November 1, 1867, Maximilian had made no attempt to disguise his hostility to his allies.

The French government having formally declined to do more than pay the auxiliary troops and the foreign legion, the distress was great, and the Imperialists, on the verge of starvation, were frequently supplied in the field by the French commissariat. Demoralization set in throughout the imperial army. Whole garrisons, receiving no pay, left their posts and turned highwaymen, even in the neighborhood of the capital.

Indeed, the desertions were now so frequent that the Liberals were able to form a "foreign legion" with the deserters of various nationalities who sought service under their flag.* Rats were leaving the sinking ship.

* See "L'Ere Nouvelle" (Mexico), September 25, 1866.

In January, 1866, the imperial army, including the Austro-Belgian legion, numbered 43,500 men. In October of the same year only 28,000 remained under arms. Many, of course, had fallen in the field, but desertion was principally accountable for this shriveling of the Mexican forces.

Permission had originally been granted French officers to take service under the imperial flag. Various army-corps had been formed, which were officered by Frenchmen as well as by Austrians and Belgians. Theoretically, a year and a half was time enough to organize the new foreign legion then well under way; but recruiting for the Mexican army was now found to be, like all other experiments successively brought to bear upon the problem, virtually impossible. Under the circumstances it seemed folly for foreign officers to enlist in the newly organized imperial regiments.

The marshal took it upon himself to withdraw the permission given some time before to French officers to pass into the Mexican service. He has been blamed for this, and accused of having deliberately hindered the organizing of Mexican forces, thus hastening the ruin of the empire. But no one not on the spot toward the close of the year 1866 can well realize the atmosphere of general sauve qui peut that prevailed in Mexico and affected all classes of society. The tide had turned. To all who had anything to lose, the only course that seemed perfectly clear was to get out of the country, leaving behind as little of their belongings as possible. Indeed, M. de Hoorickx, who remained as charge d'affaires after the departure of the Belgian minister, M. de Blondel, told me that he also was doing all in his power to prevent his countrymen from embarking upon such stormy seas.

Sober-minded Austrians, on their side, used their influence over their more adventurous comrades to prevent their remaining under the altered conditions.

And now the only hope of the empire rested upon the power of Empress Charlotte to induce the courts of Austria, Belgium, Rome, and especially the court of France, to grant a reprieve to the tottering empire by lending it further support.

To defray the expenses of her journey, thirty thousand dollars were taken from an emergency fund held as sacred for the repairs of the dikes which defend Mexico against the ever-threatening floods from the lakes, the level of which is higher than that of the city.

It soon was whispered among us that upon her arrival in Paris the Empress had not spared the marshal, and that in her interview with Napoleon III she not only had denounced him, but had asked his recall.

On September 16, 1866, the anniversary of the national independence was celebrated with unusual state by the Emperor. The Te Deum was sung in the cathedral, and a formal reception was held at the palace, where, for the last time, a large crowd assembled. After this a meeting of the council of state was held to discuss the situation.

The Liberals and Moderates had failed to strengthen the empire. As a last resort, the Emperor turned once more to the reactionary party for help. The Liberal ministers withdrew, and a new cabinet, composed of the ultra-clerical party, was formed.

Thus, at the last hour, when, without funds and abandoned by his allies, all were falling away from him, Maximilian cast his lot with the men whom, when rich in money, armies, and allies, and the future promised success, he had discarded as impossible to carry. In accepting their help he was pledging himself to factional warfare, and was virtually going back upon every declared principle which had formed the basis of his acceptance of the crown.

But in fairness it may be said that the unfortunate prince was at this time scarcely responsible for his actions. The situation was desperate. He had neither the strength nor the coolness of judgment to face the issue. His vacillating nature had been still further weakened by intermittent fever, as well as by the events of this year, so fatal to his house. The climate of Mexico did not suit him. What with malarial fever and dysentery, as well as with distracting responsibilities and cares, he was a physical wreck. Not only had he month after month felt his hopes grow faint and his throne crumble under him; not only had he every cause to lose faith in his star as well as in his own judgment: but the cannon of Lissa must have vibrated with painful distinctness through the innermost fibers of the Austrian admiral's heart, and his personal interest in Austrian affairs must have caused him to dwell with poignant regret upon his renunciation of his birthright, and his absence from the larger stage upon which, but for his wild errand, he might then have been playing a leading role.*

* See M. de Keratry, "L'Empereur Maximilien," p. 220.

The new clerical cabinet, as usual, promised to pacify the country, and to find the funds indispensable for the purpose. This was the last card of the reactionary party. Of all those involved in the issue, the clerical leaders alone had everything to lose by the downfall of the empire. Their personal interest in its prolongation was clear. With them it was a matter, if not of life and death, at least of comparative dignity and prosperity at home, or of exile and beggary abroad.

To place his fate in such hands was the last mistake of the Emperor. Such interested advisers must endeavor to cut off his retreat, when to remain must cost him his life.

The mission of the Empress abroad had, if anything, aggravated the situation. It is said that, no doubt, under the influence of the cerebral disturbance that soon afterward manifested itself, her recriminations were so violent as to arouse a feeling of personal resentment which destroyed all sympathy in Napoleon's heart. Already weary of an undertaking which from beginning to end must reflect upon his statesmanship, and which was fast becoming a reproach to the French nation, he was even then negotiating with the United States for the removal of his troops, and for the restoration of the republic.

Regardless of the onerous agreement which Maximilian only four months before had been compelled to sign, the new minister of foreign affairs, the Marquis de Moustier, on the occasion of his first reception to the diplomatic corps, on October 11, told Mr. Bigelow that the Emperor would recall the army shortly.* The minister of war had already signed a contract with Pereire, the head of the Compagnie Transatlantique, for the home passage of the last instalment of the army during the month of March.

* See letter of Mr. Bigelow to Mr. Seward, October 12 ("Diplomatic Correspondence," 1866, Part I, p. 360).

Of these fateful negotiations we, in Mexico, were then ignorant. We were under the impression that strict compliance with the terms of the recent agreement was the worst that could befall the empire. That these terms would be strictly adhered to even seemed incredible to many. There were optimists among us who thought that Napoleon's action was intended to call forth docility on the part of Maximilian and of his Mexican cabinet, and to bring them to terms. Thus it was that, although the debacle was in reality hard upon us, it yet seemed sufficiently far off not materially to affect our daily life. We therefore lightly skipped over the thin ice of our present security, unmindful of what the immediate future had in store for us.

III. COMEDY AND TRAGEDY

In the spring of 1866 our small circle was pleasantly enlarged by the arrival of the Marquis de Massa. He was the younger son of the celebrated Regnier, Duc de Massa, the able lawyer whose work upon the Code Napoleon had led him to a dukedom under Napoleon the Great.

M. de Massa was endowed with more brilliancy than perseverance. He had not passed through St. Cyr to enter the army, and had devoted much of his youth to the systematic enjoyment of life. After some of his illusions and most of his money had gone, he did as many Frenchmen of good family had done before him—he enlisted in a crack cavalry regiment of the Imperial Guard, where, after a while, thanks to mighty protectors, he exchanged his worsted stripes for gold braid and the single epaulet. He had come to Mexico in search of an excuse for rapid promotion.

Similar cases were by no means infrequent then. Michel Ney, Duc d'Elchingen, the grandson of the great marshal, when I met him in Mexico, was sergeant or corporal in a regiment of chasseurs d'Afrique, recognizable from his fellow-troopers only by his spotless linen. Shortly after this he was promoted to a sublieutenancy. His promotion was then rapid, and he did good service in the north; for although he was no reader of books and was somewhat heavy of understanding, he was as brave as his famous ancestor.*

* An officer wrote me during the Franco-Prussian war that at Rezonville, in 1870, when brilliantly charging at the head of his men, Michel Ney, then a colonel of dragoons, received three sabre-cuts over his head and face, and after killing five Prussians rolled under his wounded horse. He eventually recovered.

Count Clary, a cousin of Napoleon III, when I met him, had only recently emerged from his worsted chrysalis;** and Albert Bazaine, the marshal's own nephew, was impatiently waiting to be raised from the depressing position of a piou-piou, that he might enjoy the full social benefits of his relationship to the commander-in-chief.

* He was promoted to the rank of captain before the return of the French army, and commanded a contre-guerilla known as the "Free Company of Mexican partizans" (see D'Hericault, loc. cit., p. 79), which did brave work in the state of Michoacan against the bands of General Regules and others, and later in the neighborhood of Mexico, without ever exciting the bitter hatred which the contreguerilla of Colonel Dupin, holding the state of Vera Cruz, drew upon itself. (See "Queretaro," by Haus, p. 56.)

The position of these gentlemen in a capital where the army was, so to speak, under arms, and where no civilian's dress, therefore, was allowed to a soldier, was ambiguous and gave rise to amusing anomalies. For instance, they, of course, could not be admitted to official balls or entertainments where uniforms were de rigueur, as only officers were invited. They paid calls, however, and thus mixed on neutral ground with their officers; and so these nondescript military larvae managed to enjoy life until the day came when they might become official butterflies.

As for the Marquis de Massa, the day had long gone by when, driving in his own trap to the gate of the Paris barracks after a night spent out on leave through the leniency of General Floury, he set to work to curry his own horse. His keen wit and happy repartee, his good-humored sarcasm, and, above all, the magnetism of a personality that scorned deceit and gave itself for no better or worse than it was, combined to make him a favorite among the devotees of pleasure whom Napoleon III and Empress Eugenie had gathered about them; and notwithstanding his empty pockets, his roofless chateau in Auvergne, and his sparsely braided sleeve, he was an habitue of the Austrian embassy and of the best salons in Paris, and made for himself a conspicuous place in the innermost circle of the court of Compiegne and the Tuileries. He had written a number of light plays for the amateur stage of Parisian society, and his dramatic efforts had been interpreted by players whose high-sounding names might be found on pages of history.

His first attempt was the "Cascades de Mouchy," on December 9, 1863. The representation was given at the Chateau de Mouchy, to which "all Paris" traveled for the purpose. In the words of the "Figaro": "It was a complete mobilization of Parisian society." The Duc de Mouchy, a man of the old nobility, had recently married Princess Anna Murat; and the actors as well as the audience represented the wit, talent, wealth, and power of the Second Empire.

In collaboration with Prince de Metternich, then Austrian ambassador at the court of the Tuileries, and an amateur musician of no mean order, he had written the libretto of a ballet called "Le Roi d'Yvetot." This was given on the professional stage, but met with little success, if exception is made of the "first night," when again "all Paris" turned out to see the prince lead the orchestra, and to applaud the brilliant young author after the curtain fell.

In 1865 he wrote a revue, which was performed with great eclat before the court at Compiegne. In this really clever piece the principal occurrences of the year were touched upon and reviewed. The literary event of 1865 in France had been the publication of Napoleon's work "Les Commentaires de Cesar," and this the young courtier took as a title for his play. Once again all the wit and beauty of the court of Eugenie united to make the occasion a brilliant tribute to the imperial historian. The Comte and Comtesse de Pourtales, the Marquis and Marquise de Gallifet, the Duc and Duchesse de Mouchy, the Princesse de Sagan, the Marquis de Caux (who afterward married Adelina Patti), the Princesse de Metternich,—indeed, the elite of cosmopolis,—appeared upon the stage, and in clever verse and epigrammatic song amusingly dealt with the gossip of the day.

M. de Massa's success was mainly due to the good-natured independence of his work. He told the truth to his audience, even though it might be composed of the great of the land. He chaffed the women upon their manners, and sometimes their morals, and the men upon their idleness and their evil ways. He showed up the speculative fever which, like an epidemic, had swept over the higher ranks of Parisian society under the Second Empire.* No weakness could be sure of escaping his satire. But in dealing with all this the scalpel of the cynic was concealed under the graceful touch of the man of the world. He did not assume the tone of a moralist or of a misanthrope. He was not even an observing spectator, but a good-natured enfant du siecle, a sinner among sinners, for whom life was one long comedy.

* For instance, one stanza sung by M. de St. Maurice:

"Tout les terrains, les canaux, les carrieres,
Depuis le fer jusqu'au moindre metal,
Les champs, les eaux, les forets, les bruyeres—
Tout represente un certain capital.
Vous le voyez la fievre est generale;
Tout est matiere a speculations . . .
Tout, en effet, excepte la morale
Qu'on n'a pas mise en actions."

After the return of the Corps Expeditionnaire in 1867, when the great International Exposition was attracting to Paris the princes and celebrities of the world, "Les Commentaires de Cesar" was, at the Emperor's request, repeated at the Tuileries before the crowned heads there assembled as his guests.

Notwithstanding the seething forces underlying the brilliant surface and threatening the empire's very existence, the summer of 1867, as superficially seen in Paris, must be regarded as the very apex of Napoleon's career.

The exposition was the last and most gorgeous set piece of the many Napoleonic fireworks, the splendor of which flashed through history, and ended in the dark smoke of Sedan.

The performance at the Tuileries was one of the most select entertainments arranged at this time. The troupe of aristocratic comedians was greeted with enthusiastic applause, and the popular author received an ovation from his audience of monarchs and princes such as fate never bestowed upon Beaumarchais, Marivaux, or even Moliere!

All aglow with the excitement of his social achievements, the Marquis de Massa came to Mexico in 1866 and immediately took his place in the military household of the commander-in-chief.

As soon as he felt sufficiently posted as to the local conditions of Mexico, he went to work, and the result was a vaudeville entitled "Messieurs les Voyageurs pour Mexico, en Voiture!"

The marshal's household supplied the principal stars of the improvised dramatic company, the leader of the orchestra, a young Belgian officer, and the prima donna, an "American girl from Paris," as the Mexican papers had it, being brought in only as necessary adjuncts. Another important female part was taken by Albert Bazaine, who was turned into a superb soubrette.

The play was little more than a skit, and the plot—if the thin, sketchy incident that stood in its place may be called one—served only as an excuse for a continuous fusillade of local hits, often of a personal character. These not only kept the audience in a fever of merriment, but long afterward furnished Mexican official and social circles with topics for more or less friendly discussion. Some ill feeling and not a few unpleasant comments were, of course, the result of the little venture; and most of those concerned paid for their fun in some way or other.

The performance took place at San Cosme, at the house of the Vicomtesse de Noue. Maximilian, whose curiosity had been aroused, expressed a desire to have it repeated at the imperial palace; but having heard of certain unmerciful sallies made upon his financial decrees and other measures of his government, he did not attempt to disguise his displeasure. Of course the performance was not repeated.

No harm whatever was intended; but, looking back upon the incident, one can see that the hits, if innocently meant, coming as they did from the marshal's household, were certainly lacking in discretion. Indeed, when one considers the serious dissensions then existing between the quartier-general and the palace, it becomes clear that such jests must have had upon the court the effect of the banderillas which, in a bull-fight, by a refinement of cruelty, are stuck in the quivering flesh of the baited bull, doomed from the start, and teased to the bitter end.

Among the verses of an interminable topical song, one contained a reference to the newly organized regiment, the "Cazadores de Mejico," the recruiting of which was then taxing to the utmost Maximilian's energies:

Parmi les corps que l'on vient d'etablir
  Les Cazadors sont de tous les plus braves;
Mais, c'est egal, au moment de choisir
  J'aimerais miens m'engager dans les Zouaves!

These lines afterward assumed a strangely prophetic importance. Six months later, during the siege of Queretaro, this same regiment of Cazadores, composed of Frenchmen, Germans, and Hungarians, with about one fourth of native Mexican soldiers, was placed, with four twelve-pounders, under the command of Prince Salm-Salm. They were, according to their colonel, a wild, brawling set, constantly fighting among themselves, but ready enough to do their duty under fire.

It would seem that, after a sortie during which they had specially distinguished themselves, the Emperor visited the lines, and paused to praise their bravery. Whether or not the sting contained in M. de Massa's words had impressed them upon his mind, it is, of course, impossible to tell; but in a stirring proclamation Maximilian called them the "Zouaves of Mexico," a compliment which was received by the men with deafening shouts of enthusiasm. This account, as I read it after the final catastrophe, awoke a memory; and I found myself unconsciously humming the bit of satire upon these brave fellows, most of whom were now lying cold and stiff under the sky of Queretaro:

"Mais, c'est egal, au moment de choisir
J'aimerais mieux m'engager dans les Zouaves!"

Ah me, how closely the ridiculous here approached the sublime! How rapidly tragedy had followed upon comedy!

The first colonel of the Cazadores, Paolino Lamadrid, was in the audience that evening. He was a pleasant-looking man, noted for his great skill in the national sports, especially with the lazo. He was brave, kindly, obliging, and one of the few Mexican officers who were honestly friendly to the French. He entered into the spirit of the thing, understood the joke, and took no offense. He had lent for the occasion his Mexican dress, sombrero, chapareras, etc., for the character of a Mexicanized French colonist who, after a series of Mexican adventures, had returned to France and to his family laden with Mexican millions.

Colonel Paolino Lamadrid did not live to stand by his sovereign in the last heroic hour of the empire. He was killed early in January, in an unimportant engagement at Cuernavaca, one of Maximilian's favorite residences, situated some fifty miles from Mexico, and which had already fallen into the hands of the Juarists.

Colonel Lamadrid was ordered to recapture the town. He fell into an ambush, and after a brave struggle was shot down. His troops held their ground, and before retreating next day they recovered his body, which had been badly mutilated and was only identified by his fine and silky black beard, which formed one of his most striking features.* It is said that one of the early hallucinations of the unfortunate Empress, on her way to Rome, was that she saw Colonel Lamadrid lurking about, disguised as an organ-grinder.

* D'Hericault, pp. 82, 83.

But to return to this now historic entertainment. The general situation was summed up finally in a serio-comic manner in a song which, if it then brought down the house, afterward drew severe criticism upon the thoughtless heads of author and performers:

Oui, cette terre
Hospitaliere
Un jour sera, c'est moi qui vous le dis,
Pour tout le monde
L'arche feconde
Des gens de coeur et des colons hardis.
  Que faut-il donc pour cesser nos alarmes?
De bons soldats et de bons generaux,
  De bons prefets et surtout des gendarmes,
Des financiers et des gardes ruraux.

Refrain:
Allons courage,
Vite a l'ouvrage;
  La France est la pour nous preter secours.
Vieux incredules,
Sots ridicules,
  De nos travaux n'entravez pas le cours.

This song, pledging France to back up Mexican enterprise in every venture, may serve to show how ignorant all were at this time of the sudden determination taken by the Tuileries to set aside the agreement of July 30, 1866, and to put an immediate end to the intervention.

It was written by a member of the marshal's military household, and the refrain was sung by a chorus of the marshal's officers, in the presence of the marshal himself, and of a large audience composed of French, Austrian, and Belgian officers, as well as of members of the imperial government, on September 26, 1866, i.e., just at the time when General Castelnau, who landed at Vera Cruz on October 10, was starting on his mission, the object of which was to force the abdication of Maximilian, and to bring about the winding up of the empire and the immediate return of the army.

At this very time, it will be remembered, a contract was being entered upon by the French government with the house of Pereire, which was to furnish immediate home transportation for the French army.*

* Bigelow, letter to Seward, October 12, 1866.

The song was not meant to be the cruel jest which it must have seemed to those about the Mexican Emperor who were better informed with regard to

Napoleon's negotiations with the government of the United States. By those whose all was at stake it must have been taken for a wanton insult.

Indeed, society in Mexico was not just then in the right frame of mind to appreciate M. de Massa's witticisms. Even among his own friends they proved singularly infelicitous.

The displeasure of Madame la Marechale, whose youth and beauty were then superior to her sense of humor, was aroused by a verse the timeworn wit of which she seemed unable to appreciate, and in which she saw an insult to her people:

Le roi Henri, qui detestait l'impot,
Des Mexicains aurait bien fait l'affaire,
Au lieu de poule, un zopilote an pot:
Voila l'moyen de devenir populaire!

The zoplote, although protected by law as a scavenger, is held as unclean by the Mexicans, who would almost starve rather than eat it; and the suggestion, taken seriously and indignantly resented by Mme. Bazaine, created quite a ripple of disturbance in the marshal's family.

The following incident also swelled the ranks of M. de Massa's French critics:

Before the performance gossip had been busy with it, and its source had partly been traced to Colonel Petit, a good enough friend, but who at the time happened to be chafing under the sting of a practical joke, recently played upon him by some of his comrades, in which M. de Massa had had a share.

During the recent campaign made by the marshal in the interior, with a view to the concentration of the army preparatory to its retreat, Colonel Petit, with his regiment, arrived at a small town, the authorities of which prepared to receive the French with due honor. Eager for fun, his comrades confidentially disclosed to the alcalde the fact that Colonel Petit was a great personage—indeed, no less than the son of the celebrated General Petit whom Napoleon, about to depart for Elba, and taking leave of his veterans, had singled out and embraced as the representative of the Grande Armee.

I do not remember whether the mischievous wags suggested to the alcalde, a pure Indian wearing sombrero, shirt, and white calzoneras, a repetition of the solemn scene of Fontainebleau, or whether the worthy Indian evolved the notion unaided; but the result was that poor Colonel Petit, much against his will, found himself forced into playing a parody of his father's part to the alcalde's Napoleon. In the presence of his men, amid the jeers and cheers of his amused comrades, he had to submit to the speech and public accolade of the worthy magistrate.

The perpetrators of this pleasantry did not soon allow him to forget it. It long remained a sore thing with him; and as he allowed his resentment to appear, an extra verse was on the day of the performance added, for his benefit, to the principal topical song:

A Mexico les cancans vont leur train,
  On vous condamne avant de vous entendre,
C'est bien "petit" d'ereinter son prochain,
  Bon entendeur saura bien nous comprendre.

As this was sung the audience laughingly turned toward him—a fact which did not tend to make him more amiably disposed, although he bowed gracefully enough, and pretended to enjoy the fun.

Altogether, the play, if more than a success as a performance, added nothing to the popularity of the quartier-general. It, however, created far more comment than its literary merit warranted—if this may be said, without detracting from the credit of the author, who himself, looking back upon it later in his career, said that it read as though it had been "written on a drum."

Sadowa had been fought and lost; but it would have been difficult, to make out from their attitude whether or not the sympathies of the officers of the Corps Expeditionnaire were honestly with their Austrian allies. Strangely enough, the news had been received by them as though it involved no serious warning to France. The full significance of the new mode of warfare, of the needle-gun and other new implements of war, was obscured in their eyes by their naive Jingoism. The French officers in those days underrated all other nations; and even the superior armament and discipline of the Germans, as exhibited in that short campaign, failed to impress them as they should. They sang:

L'aiguille est un outil
  Dont je ne suis en peine
  Tant que j'aurai la mienne [the bayonet]
Au bout de mon fusil.
  Vous qui ehantez victoire,
Heros de Sadowa,
  Rappelez-vous l'histoire
D'Auerstadt et d'Iena.

Alas! the time was drawing near when the cannon of Reichshofen was to change the merry tune of the French chanson into a dirge for many of the brave, light-hearted fellows, then so unmindful of the storm slowly gathering in the east.

The pomp and dignity of the court had vanished, and social life in the capital no longer centered about the imperial palace.

Even previous to the departure of the Empress, the Monday receptions had been discontinued, without their loss being seriously felt. At best they had never been other than dull, formal affairs. The ball-room was a large hall, always insufficiently lighted, and narrowed in the middle by the platform where stood the imperial throne under a canopy of velvet. Here, after their new guests had been officially presented in an adjoining hall, the Emperor and Empress took their seat. Before supper they made a solemn tour of the ball-room. The dancing then ceased, and the crowd stood in chilled expectancy, and made way for them, each in turn receiving from them, as they passed, a smile, a nod, or some commonplace word of greeting.

Maximilian was happy in his remarks on such occasions. Naturally affable and kindly, like most princes trained to this sort of thing, his memory for names and faces was remarkable. We were presented at court on the first of the imperial fortnightly Mondays, and with us, of course, the larger number of the guests present; and yet, some weeks later, when making his tour of the ball-room, the Emperor stopped before us, and inquired about an absent member of the family, apparently placing us exactly. Many other instances of his memory and power of observation in such small matters were related by others.

He was tall, slight, and handsome, although the whole expression of his face revealed weakness and indecision. He looked, and was, a gentleman. His dignity was without hauteur. His manner was attractive; he had the faculty of making you feel at ease; and he possessed far more personal magnetism than did the Empress.

Hers was a strong, intelligent face, the lines of which were somewhat hard at times; and her determined expression impressed one with the feeling that she was the better equipped of the two to cope intelligently with the difficulties of practical life. It is probable that, had she been alone, she might have made a better attempt at solving the problems than did Maximilian; at least such was Marshal Bazaine's opinion, as expressed before me on one occasion, during her brief regency, when she had shown special firmness and clear judgment in dealing with certain complicated state affairs.

She, however, was reserved, somewhat lacking in tact and adaptability; and a certain haughtiness of manner, a dignity too conscious of itself, at first repelled many who were disposed to feel kindly toward her. It is more than likely that under this proud mien she concealed a suffering spirit, or, at least, the consciousness of a superiority that must efface itself. Who will ever know the travail of her proud heart and the prolonged strain under which her mind finally succumbed! For notwithstanding the prudence and decided ability with which she had conducted the difficult affairs of the realm during the Emperor's absence in 1864, it was hinted that on his return she was allowed little weight in public affairs, and that her advice when given was seldom followed. After her departure even the semblance of a court disappeared.

On the other hand, the quartier-general had lost much of its animation since the marshal's second marriage. His first union had been childless, and his delight in the joys and cares of a tardy paternity absorbed all the leisure left him by the military and other responsibilities of his position.

Indeed, the growing ill feeling existing in political circles was spreading rapidly, gradually destroying good fellowship. A tragic incident resulting in the death of a brave French officer, Colonel Tourre (May, 1865), stirred French circles to their very depths.

One night a house was on fire. A lieutenant and some Zouaves of the Third Regiment went in to save property. As the flames grew in intensity the colonel arrived on the scene, and realizing the danger of his men, rushed in to help and direct them. Shortly after he entered, the floor on which he stood gave way, and the unfortunate man was plunged into a fiery grave. The men managed to escape from the building, but the lieutenant and one Zouave were horribly burned, and died in a few hours. The impression made upon society was profound. Every one turned out for the funeral.

The marshal and his staff, on foot and bareheaded under the tropical sun, followed the remains, and did them as much honor as though the dead had been of the highest rank. It so happened, however, that the cortege, upon its passage, was insulted by some ruffians in the crowd, and the incident aroused more indignation and national feeling on both sides than the strictly limited nature of the incident warranted. One of the offenders, a student, was apprehended, and the clemency of Maximilian, who forthwith pardoned him, was regarded as a deliberate insult at French headquarters.

Another incident, equally limited in its origin, produced a still more serious scandal among the allies, as it gave rise to a report that the Austrians and the French quartered at Puebla were actually coming to blows. One morning a party of Austrians, one of whom was Count de la Sala, entered the Hotel de las Diligencias at Puebla. Some Frenchmen were present. One of these, a sergeant, taking umbrage at the count's manner, became surly, and called him ANIMAL, whereupon the young Austrian slapped him in the face. Others interfered, and the Frenchman left the room. Presently, however, he returned, holding a revolver in his hand, and walked threateningly toward the count, who, anticipating the attack, jumped upon him, and, seizing his arm, made the weapon useless. The sergeant, bent upon avenging the blow received, then struck at the count with his free hand, on which he wore a set of brass knuckles, inflicting an ugly gash over the left eye. Things were getting serious for the count. His companions were keeping watch at the door to prevent interference from the outside and to see fair play. The bystanders had fled. Blood was streaming down his face, almost blinding him. The sergeant struck at him a second time, when the count drew his sword and ran him through the body. There was now no suppressing the affair, which caused a profound sensation. The first reports that reached the capital magnified the occurrence into something very like a riot, and on both sides the real bitterness of the feeling so long suppressed blazed forth for a time undisguised.

Indeed, it is only recently that, meeting the count in Egypt, I heard from him how very limited the incident was. Count de la Sala, who afterward entered the service of the Khedive and now lives in Cairo, still bears the mark of the Frenchman's brass knuckles upon his forehead. In 1866 the irritation had reached such a point that Maximilian, disregarding the feelings of his allies, gave a pension to the widow of General Zaragoza, the hero of the "Cinco de Mayo." This act of the monarch for whose cause the battle had been fought by them was not unnaturally regarded as a wanton insult by the French.

Society now scarcely deserved the name, and the sociability of the capital was confined to small groups of people who privately met for enjoyment in the most informal manner.

A number of officers had invited their wives to join them in Mexico, and among them were some charming and clever women, such as the Comtesse de Courcy, the Vicomtesse de Noue, and Mme. Magnan, who by throwing open their salons greatly contributed to the general enjoyment.

Other women of various nationalities formed a background to these, and added to the local interest. One of them afterward played a conspicuous part in the closing scene of the empire. Prince Salm-Salm and his handsome American wife came to Mexico in 1866. They found serious difficulty in gaining admittance into either the social or the official circles of the capital. The relations of Prussia with Austria were anything but cordial at the time; and soon after their arrival the war broke out which culminated at Sadowa. A Prussian subject, the prince was naturally looked upon with distrust by the Austrians, who showed him scant respect. He had brought letters from Baron Gerold, the Prussian minister at Washington; from Baron de Wydenbruck, the Austrian minister; and from the Marquis de Montholon: but these seemed unable to win for him even a hearing from the Emperor.

The French, on the other hand, had little sympathy with a German prince who, having hired his sword to the republic of the United States, had now come in search of a new allegiance, to offer his services to imperial Mexico's Austrian ruler.

When, six months after his arrival in Mexico, the most unremitting efforts on his part at last obtained for him a commission, and he was given (July,

1866) the rank of colonel in the auxiliary corps—under General Neigre, he was treated with no special cordiality. He then applied to the minister of war for permission to pass into the Belgian corps. From this time he and his attractive wife obscurely followed the fortunes of Colonel Van der Smissen, whose personal regard they had won, until the withdrawal of the French and the Austro-Belgian armies, by clearing the stage for the last scene, brought them in full relief, under the search-light of history, by the side of the imperial victim.

At the time of which I now speak, the princess, as well as her husband, had donned the silver and gray of the Belgian regiment, and cheerfully shared the fatigues and dangers of camp life in war time—like a soldadera, contemptuously said her proud sisters in society; for this mode of existence naturally drew upon her the criticism of the more conventional of her sex in the Mexican colony. But for all that, she and her husband bravely stood by the Emperor to the bitter end, when older and more valued, though less courageous, friends had dropped away, and had left him, stripped of the imperial purple, to struggle for existence, an adventurer among adventurers.

IV. GENERAL CASTELNAU

The denouement was drawing near. On October 10 General Castelnau landed in Vera Cruz, on a special mission from Napoleon III. He was accompanied by the Comte de St. Sauveur, his officier d'ordonnance, and by the Marquis de Gallifet.

His arrival created considerable excitement and some anxiety, not only at the palace, where Maximilian was expecting news from France much as a man awaits his sentence, but also at the quartier-general.

Information had come that the course taken by the marshal had not proved satisfactory to Napoleon. It was whispered that he had not shown sufficient zeal in the task required of him under the new policy; that his sovereign was seriously annoyed at what he conceived to be wilful procrastination in the withdrawal of the army; and that he was now sending his own aide-de-camp to cut the Gordian knot in the tangled skein of Mexican politics.

The marshal's popularity in his command was no longer what it had been. The intrigues carried on both in France and in Mexico, with the purpose of setting up General Douay in his place, had resulted in ill feeling that had been turned to account by the Mexican Imperialists.

There were those in the army who did not fear to impute unworthy motives to the commander-in-chief's actions. His Mexican marriage had not added to his prestige among the French. It was hinted that his lenient dealings with the empire and with Maximilian were due to the fact that the handsome property at San Cosme must be left behind in the event of his return to France; and even worse calumnies, too ill founded to mention, were circulated with regard to the selfishness of his policy.

The fact that General Castelnau, who found himself intrusted with superior powers, extending, if necessary, even to the actual superseding of the commander-in-chief, was, from the military standpoint, the marshal's subordinate, seemed likely to add considerably to the chance of new difficulties.

Meanwhile the general seemed in no hurry to enter upon his thankless mission. Unmindful of the natural suspense of those who were awaiting him, he and his little party traveled leisurely. A martyr to the gout, he lingered on his way, no doubt making good use of his time as he went for the study of the situation which he was called upon to clear up. A fortnight thus elapsed before he approached the capital.

Serious events had taken place during his journey from the coast which at first seemed somewhat to simplify the difficulties of his mission; and upon his arrival in the capital affairs had reached an acute crisis which men cleverer than himself and his colleagues, working in harmony, might perhaps have turned to favorable account for France.

On October 18, three days before General Castelnau reached the capital, a telegram, sent from Miramar via New York by the Comte de Bombelles, brought to Chapultepec the news of the illness of Empress Charlotte. This last blow fell with crushing weight upon the suffering Emperor. This was about the time when the return of the Empress was expected, and he had made his plans to travel toward the coast to meet her on her homeward journey. Some days earlier Colonel Kodolitch and his Austrian hussars had been summoned to the capital to form his body-guard. Maximilian now at once resolved to leave Chapultepec, and to retire to Orizaba.

As soon as this was known, an uneasy feeling spread over Mexico caused by a rumor that the empire was at an end, and that Maximilian was leaving the city, never to return. The result was a panic. The new cabinet and other clerical loaders flocked to the castle to get some assurance as to the Emperor's intentions; but he was ill, and denied himself to all visitors, even to the Princess Iturbide, who, it is said,* resented the slight in violent language.**

* See Basch, "Maximilien en Mexique," p. 56.

** In 1866, the imperial couple being childless, Maximilian bethought himself of establishing a dynasty. One of the Emperor Iturbide's sons, Angel, was married to an American woman, and his child, a mere infant, became the basis of a remarkable agreement which excited much comment.

By the terms of this contract, and for certain important pecuniary considerations, the uncles, aunt, and father of the boy agreed that the Iturbide family, including the parents, should leave the country, and that Maximilian should become the guardian of the child, the aunt, Dona Josefa Iturbide, the masterful mind of the family, remaining as his governess. The consent of the mother was wrenched from her, and the contract was duly signed. Its execution was not carried out without considerable resistance on the part of Princess Iturbide who, however, was finally sent out of the country.

The ministers, terror-stricken at the thought of being left alone to face a revolution, tendered their resignation in a body; and Senor Lares declared that if the Emperor left the city there would no longer be a government.

Looking back upon the event, it would now seem that by threatening the ministers with summary measures if they did not reconsider their decision, Marshal Bazaine had lost his one opportunity to clear the tables for a new "deal," and thus become master of the situation. But it is only fair to state that the conditions were bewildering. The concentration of the army had not been perfected, and scattered detachments were still at considerable distances. Rumors of Sicilian Vespers once more floated in the air. The exasperation of the clerical party against the French was now far more violent than that of the Liberals. Indeed, it seemed difficult to calculate the extent of the conflagration which a single spark might kindle. Moreover, no one then doubted Maximilian's resolve to abdicate. To-day, however, it would seem that by stemming the torrent at this time Marshal Bazaine defeated his own end. This may fairly be inferred from the part played by the priest Fischer in the transaction.

Father Fischer was an obscure adventurer of low degree, and of more than shady reputation, whose shrewdness and talent for intrigue had impressed themselves upon the weakened mind of the Emperor in the latter days of his reign. Utterly unscrupulous, with everything to gain for himself and his party, and with absolutely nothing to lose but a life which he took good care to save by avoiding danger, he insinuated himself into the confidence of Maximilian, and became the Mephistopheles of the last act in the Mexican drama. Having but recently risen to the confidential position he now occupied near the person of the Emperor, the latter's abdication was obviously against his interests. When the ministers threatened to resign, he is stated to have represented to them that their action was likely to precipitate the catastrophe which they sought to avoid; that by such a demonstration of their own helplessness they must only confirm the Emperor's determination; and he persuaded them that it the Emperor were not allowed temporarily to retire to Orizaba he might without further delay return to Europe.

It is claimed by Dr. Basch* that the priest's arguments had as much to do with bringing the ministers to resume their portfolios as the marshal's firmness. However this may be, the crisis was avoided. On October 2, Maximilian, Senor Arroyo, Father Fischer, Dr. Basch, and Councilor Hertzel, under the escort of Colonel Kodolitch and his Austro-Hungarian regiment, started from Chapultepec at three o'clock in the morning. There was no doubt in any one's mind that his departure for Orizaba was the first relay in the Emperor's journey to the coast.

* See Basch, loc. cit., p. 61.

There is something profoundly pathetic in this chapter of his life. It forms a fitting introduction to that tragedy the threatening outline of which even then faintly appeared upon the horizon as a dreadful possibility.

The friends whose society had enlivened the earlier days of his reign in his adopted land were now scattered like straws at the first approach of the cyclone. The Empress had gone upon her hopeless mission, never to return; and the faithful Comte de Bombelles was with her to advise and protect. Court and political intrigues had loosened the bond that had united the Emperor to the great clerical leaders who had made the empire.

Whatever his dreams may have been, the reality was pitiful. The gilding thinly spread over the Mexican crown had worn off; the glitter had disappeared. The treasury was empty, courtiers were now few, and the successor of the Montezumas, the descendant of the Hapsburgs, the popular archduke, the Austrian admiral, was now reduced to the intimacy of a corrupt adventurer in priestly garb, who had stolen into his confidence upon the shortest acquaintance, and of his German physician, Dr. Basch, whom he had known only one month. These two, with his still faithful followers, the councilor Hertzel and the naturalist Bilimek, were his only confidential advisers during the terrible crisis upon the issue of which depended life and fame.

It so happened that, a day or two after the Emperor's departure, as we were passing Chapultepec on horseback, a friend invited us to enter the palace to look at the costly improvements made in the last two years by the Emperor. While there we were shown the private apartments. No one had as yet straightened out the place. A certain disorder still reigned, as though the imperial inmate had just left. His clothes hung in open closets, and the condition of the rooms betokened a hasty departure, and formed a dramatic mise en scene for the opening of the last act of his life.

A coincidence brought General Castelnau and his party to Ayotla, on their way to the capital, as the Emperor and his escort stopped there for breakfast. Maximilian, however, refused to see the envoy. It is said that he even declined to see Captain Pierron, his own secretary, then traveling with the general.

At this time the unfortunate prince seemed utterly crushed under the repeated blows dealt him by fate. According to his physician, then his daily companion, his imagination shoved him his own conduct as a noble effort to regenerate the country by the establishment of an empire resting upon the will of the nation. This effort had been frustrated "by the resistance of the Mexicans [!] and the vexations of the French."

The journey was a dreary one. The Emperor most of the time remained silent. On the way he generally accepted the hospitality of priests.

A certain apprehension was felt as to his safety, and the road was well guarded, as it was feared that he might be kidnapped. That such fears were not wholly unfounded was proved by an incident which took place at Aculzingo. After a short halt, when the imperial party was about to proceed on its journey, it was discovered with dismay that the eight white mules forming the Emperor's team had been stolen.

At Orizaba he received his last ovation; but these public demonstrations had lost their charm. He withdrew to the house of Senor Bringas, a violent reactionary, most inimical to the French. There he denied himself to every one. Of his military household he retained only two Mexican officers—Colonel Ormachea and Colonel Lamadrid. Later he retired to the hacienda of Jalapilla. While here even letters were not sure to reach him. His correspondence passed through interested hands, and was sifted under prying eyes, before being placed before him. No one was allowed to see him without the knowledge of the priest, who was rapidly obtaining over him an influence that was to lead him to his death. Those who approached him at this time reported him as completely under the influence, almost in the custody, of Father Fischer.

So complete was his mental collapse that it was said, and by some believed, that during their residence at Cuernavaca, prior to the departure of the Empress, a subtle poison known to the Indians of that region, and the action of which was through the brain, had been administered to the imperial couple.*

* An attempt is said to have been made upon his life in July, 1866. The affair was hushed up, but is said to have made a deep impression on his mind. See D'Hericault, "Maximilien et le Mexique: Histoire des Derniers Mois de l'Empire du Mexique," pp. 29, 54.

The condition of the Empress, the prolonged fits of depression to which Maximilian was subject when he resolved to remove his residence to Orizaba, away from the presence of his hated allies, his extreme listlessness, which betrayed itself in the carelessness of his attire and in his lapses of etiquette and of memory, gave color to the report. But there was quite enough in the unfortunate prince's situation to account for the abnormal condition of his mind without having recourse to romantic fancies.

All this time the Austrian frigate Elizabeth was at anchor off Vera Cruz, awaiting his pleasure, ready to take him back to Trieste, and part of his baggage was already on board.

His own countrymen looked upon the game as lost. The empire, which for some time had been caving in at the center, was now everywhere crumbling at the edges. Only the most unblushing personal interest could advise, and the most inconsistent folly consider, the retaining of a crown which, under circumstances even less inauspicious, he had only a short time before wisely resolved to surrender.

Unsuccessful in his attempt to govern with French financial and military support, how could he contemplate reigning alone, without allies, money, or credit? The mere thought seemed madness. After insisting upon a plebiscite to sanction his reign, how could he honorably remain now that the country in arms was everywhere falling away from his standard?

On November 6 the rumor of his abdication was circulated in New York; and the London "Post" and "Star" published it as a fact. But intrigue and folly prevailed.

It has been claimed that a communication from his former secretary, the Belgian Eloin, now his agent abroad, had a decisive effect upon his final resolution. In this letter, since published by M. de Keratry, M. Eloin warned Maximilian against affording the French an easy way out of their difficulties by yielding to General Castelnau's wiles. He urged upon the Emperor the maintaining of the empire after the departure of the foreigners, a free appeal to the Mexican nation for the material means of sustaining himself, and, in case of failure, the return of the crown to the people who gave it. Thus, and thus alone, in the opinion of the secretary, could the Emperor return with credit to Europe, with an untarnished fame, and "play the part which belonged to him in every respect in the important events that could not fail to occur" in Austria.

The hints at the general dissatisfaction with the present order of things at home, at the discouragement of Emperor Francis Joseph, at the popularity of Maximilian both in his native country and in Venetia, show that, in the mind of his secretary at least, the possibilities of Maximilian's political career were by no means confined to the sovereignty of Mexico. In reading this remarkable letter, one's mind involuntarily turns to the family scene enacted at Miramar, when Maximilian, compelled by his brother to renounce his rights to the Austrian throne, clung to them with a tenacity that seriously loosened the close bond that hitherto had united the two men.

This letter also explains the insistence of Francis Joseph, through his ambassador Baron de Lago, when the possibility of his brother's return was discussed, that Maximilian, once upon Austrian soil, should drop the imperial title.* However this may be, from this time Maximilian's mind seemed made up. He determined to risk his all upon the promises of the clerical leaders.

* Compare "L'Empire de Maximilien," M. de Keratry, p. 220. vol. iii, p. 404) It has been stated by M. Domenech ("Histoire du Mexique," that Maximilian's mother also wrote an urgent letter, advising him not to return to Europe yet.

General Castelnau and his party arrived in the capital on October 21,1866. A few days after their arrival, Mme. Magnan invited a number of us to take supper at her house, after the opera, to meet the newcomers.

The general was a tall, middle-aged man of prepossessing mien and soldierly bearing. A charming talker, his manners were those of one accustomed to the best society. He readily fell into our easy life.

He constantly invited us to his box at the opera, and at first arranged pleasant parties; but later, when the gravity of the situation weighed upon him, and his health suffered under it, while he often placed the box at our disposal, he came to it only when equal to the exertion.

Notwithstanding many admirable qualities, the general was scarcely strong enough for the part which he was called upon to play. Indeed, it is difficult to imagine how any representative of the Emperor of the French, at this stage, could have assumed control of events. Looking back upon it now, it would seem as though, under existing conditions, arbitration alone could have stemmed the current of human passion then hurrying all involved toward the final catastrophe.

The knowledge that Napoleon III, who had set up his throne, was now in accord with the United States government and with the Liberal leaders to tear it from under him, stung Maximilian to the quick. He not unnaturally felt a strong desire to remain a stumbling-block in the way of negotiations which to him seemed treacherous and infamous. When General Castelnau arrived he was hesitating. The presence of Napoleon's aide-de-camp was not calculated to soothe his feelings. The return of General Miramon and General Marquez at this crisis again turned the tide of events.

These men, formerly set aside through French influence, felt a resentment which added strength to their party feeling. The confidence of the Emperor in their ability once more to rally the people about his banner, through the influence of the clergy, triumphed over his indecision. Senor Lares had promised him the immediate control of four million dollars and of an army ready to take the field. Now here were old, experienced leaders to take command.

He hesitated no longer. Breaking with all declared principles of policy, he threw himself into the arms of the clerical party, and pledging himself to reinstate the clergy and to return to the church its confiscated property, prepared to play his last hand without the French.

The marshal was anxiously awaiting the promised documents which were to announce the final terms of abdication. Instead of these, Colonel Kodolitch was sent by the Emperor to arrange the preliminary details for the return of the Austro-Belgian troops. The letter announcing his arrival (October 31) was, moreover, sufficiently ambiguous in its wording to leave Maximilian a loophole by which to escape from his former declared intention. The negotiations were now opened anew. A meeting of the council of state was called at Jalapilla, to which the marshal was summoned, "to consider the establishment of a stable government to protect the interests that might be compromised," etc. The French government had, however, already come to an understanding with the United States, and the French agents in Mexico deemed it best that the marshal should not be present.

After a three days' session, the meeting at Orizaba resulted in a plan of action calculated to bring about a complete rupture between Maximilian and his former allies.

On December 1 Maximilian issued his official manifesto, in which he announced his intention to call together a national congress, and his determination, upon the representations of his council and his ministers, to remain at the head of affairs.

When Cortez, after landing upon the coast of Mexico, decided to burn his ships, he did not more thoroughly cut off his retreat than did Maximilian when, throwing himself into the hands of the reactionaries, he wrote his final letter to Marshal Bazaine, and published his manifesto. All personal relations now virtually ceased between the Emperor and the marshal. Official communications were carried on through the president of the council of state.

On the very day when the imperial proclamation was issued, General Sherman and Messrs. Lewis, Plumb, and Campbell arrived in the port of Vera Cruz, on board of the Susquehanna. The event caused genuine surprise.

A few days before their arrival, the marshal had received from the Marquis de Montholon a notice of their departure on a mission having for its object the reinstatement of the government of Juarez without conflict with the French, the abdication of Maximilian being then regarded as a fact.

General Magruder, who met the American envoys in Havana, reported to them that at the date of his departure from Mexico, on November 1, Maximilian was on the eve of retiring; that he had been detained at Orizaba only by the arrival of Generals Miramon and Marquez; and that the common understanding was that the government had been handed over to Marshal Bazaine.

The American consul, Mr. Otterburg, called upon the commander-in-chief, and told him that his government was acting in concert with the Tuileries to restore the republic, and that General Porfirio Diaz was the leader into whose hands the care of the capital should be transferred in order to avoid possible bloodshed. He therefore urged upon the marshal the expediency of inviting General Diaz to advance near to the city. According to M. de Keratry, Mr. Otterburg even informed him that arrangements had been made with the bankers of the capital to assure one month's pay to the troops of the Liberal leader. This episode plainly illustrates the lack of concert and of mutual understanding so characteristic of every attempt made at this time by the French leaders at home and abroad to steer out of the cruel position in which the national honor had been placed.

The unlooked-for result of his negotiations was a severe blow to General Castelnau. He had not once been summoned to the Emperor's presence, and the principal object of his mission had utterly failed. The gravity of the situation, as well as its annoyances, weighed upon him, and he was ill and depressed.

A last attempt was made by the French representatives, on December 8, to demonstrate to Maximilian, in a joint note, the impossibility of sustaining himself without the French army. General Castelnau announced to him that the return of the troops would take place during the first months of 1867. A few days later (December 13) the effect of this communication was heightened by a despatch from Napoleon III, then at Compiegne, peremptorily ordering the return of the foreign legion.

By the treaty of Miramar, the services of the legion were insured to Maximilian for six years; but what did Napoleon then care for treaties!

General Castelnau made one more personal effort to save the situation. Accompanied by M. Dano* and the Comte de St. Sauveur, he started on December 20 for Puebla, where Maximilian was the guest of the archbishop of the diocese.

* A strong feeling existed against M. Dano, the French minister, who was openly accused of selfishness in his policy. He had married a young Mexican woman, whose rich dowry was derived from the mines of Real del Monte,

and it was urged by the Imperialists that his weight was cast in the scales on the side of the Juarists, with a view to safeguarding his Mexican interests.

According to a note received by me from one of the travelers, they were at first sanguine of success, so impossible did it seem that the Emperor would seriously persevere in his resolve. But although they remained several days, and did their utmost to win over the Emperor's Mexican advisers, nothing came of this supreme attempt.* They were reluctantly admitted to an audience by Maximilian. In the course of this interview he recognized the fact that he probably must leave Mexico, but declared himself the best judge of the proper time for him to lay down his crown, and claimed the right to turn over the reins of government to the administration that must succeed the empire.

* Father Fischer, it is said, was offered thirty thousand dollars to urge Maximilian to abdicate. (D'Hericault, p. 39).

Little show of good feeling existed now between Napoleon's special envoy and the quartier-general. Indeed, the lack of harmony was spreading to officers of lesser rank. Severe criticism was indulged in on both sides. Never was the cynical old French saying so fully borne out by fact: "Quand il n'y a pas de foin au ratelier, les chevaux se battent." There was no success or even honorable failure possible; and the racked brains of the leaders found relief in unjust blame of one another, and in mutual accusations, which served only to lower the plane to which the great impending disaster must fall in the eyes of posterity.

The alluring mirage of a neo-Latin empire had completely vanished from the Western horizon. Where it had stood, the dissatisfied French army, under inharmonious leaders, now saw only a heavy bank of clouds and every sign of the approaching storm.

It will be remembered* that as a result of the new agreement with France, signed by Maximilian July 30, 1866, mixed regiments had been formed with the debris of the disbanded auxiliary corps and with liberated French soldiers. It had originally been intended to form with the Cazadores de Mejico an effective force of fifteen thousand men, to which it was planned to add ten regiments of cavalry. The first of these was commanded by Colonel Lopez. In December, 1866, three companies of gendarmes, numbering in all some twelve hundred men, were organized under Colonel Tindal. A regiment of red hussars, composed of the debris of the disbanded Austrian hussars and uhlans, about seven hundred men, was placed under the command of Captain Khevenhuller;** and this, with the Austrian regiment of Colonel Hammerstein,*** completed the new organization. A large number of Frenchmen, the best of whom had been detached from the military service with the official sanction of their government, had thus entered the imperial army and received from the Mexican government their equipment and the advertised premium offered. They had formed the framework and backbone of the new regiments, for the equipment of which Maximilian had strained every nerve, going so far as to sacrifice even his own silver plate.

* See above, "foreign legion."
** Now Prince Khevenhuller.

*** Colonel Hammerstein was killed in the trenches during the siege of Mexico on May 25, 1867. He commanded the defense of the western approach to the city by Vallejo and San Lazaro, as well as Peralvillo to the north, facing Guadalupe, In his defense of the latter position he was supported by General O'Horan, who was at a later date taken and put to death by order of President Juarez.

In the beginning of January, 1867, the marshal, under orders received from Paris, issued a circular withdrawing the consent of the French government to these enlistments, and offering to all such enlisted soldiers and officers the means of returning to France. A few days later, on the 11th, this offer was extended to all French subjects, and even to the Austro-Belgian auxiliaries should they wish to avail themselves of it.

In his circular the marshal recalled the law which deprives any Frenchman serving under a foreign flag of his rights as a French citizen. This placed in the position of deserters French soldiers and officers who in good faith had accepted service in the new Mexican army. It practically forced them to break their oath of allegiance to Maximilian, and to despoil the treasury of the premium received and already spent, or to become outlaws in the eyes of their own country. The false position in which these men were placed was, a few weeks later, cruelly emphasized when General Escobedo, after his victory over Miramon at San Jacinto, took advantage of the legal quibble thus offered him, and caused French prisoners to be shot as declared outlaws under Marshal Bazaine's circular. Notwithstanding all this, out of the remainder of the Cazadores a battalion was formed, and eventually placed under the command of Prince Salm-Salm, and later under that of the Austrian commander Pitner. These did magnificent service at Queretaro.*

* See above, "Cazadores de Mejico."

After the departure of the French army, an effective force of some five hundred men was organized of French deserters and such Frenchmen as, for some cause or other, had remained in Mexico. This formed a contre-guerilla, which, under the orders of Commandant Chenet, eventually did good service in the defense of Mexico. But the marshal's circular, by removing the better element among the officers of the newly enrolled corps, ruthlessly broke up the organization of the little army of twenty thousand men so laboriously collected by Maximilian, and became the latter's bitterest and perhaps best-founded grievance against his former allies.

Urged by General Castelnau, the marshal was steadily concentrating his troops. The foreign representatives were fast leaving the country. Unmistakable symptoms of a final collapse were everywhere visible, and all who had been in any way conspicuous in their sympathy with the intervention or the empire were anxiously preparing for the catastrophe.

V. THE END OF THE FRENCH INTERVENTION

The cheerfulness of the imperial capital had faded away in the suspense and anxiety of the moment. All wore grave, anxious faces. Those who were going first were busy and bustling. The Mexicans whom one met in the street looked sullen and often hateful. It did not seem safe freely to express one's opinions; but thoughtful people felt that the close of the intervention, if it did not carry with it that of the empire, opened up possibilities that one shuddered to contemplate. Young and old, Mexicans and foreigners, realized that they were playing a part in the opening scene of the last act of a tragedy the denouement of which no one dared to guess.

A serious personal problem was now before us. What were we to do? Closely connected as we had been with the invaders, we could expect little favor. Nor could we even depend upon the protection of the United States flag, as the Imperialists would for some time, at least, remain in possession of the capital. Yet to leave Mexico was a serious step for us to take; it meant abandoning considerable property, and at such a time this meant its loss.

The matter was decided for us at military headquarters. Our friends were clear that the future was too uncertain for any one to remain who had in any great degree been connected with the intervention. All earnestly urged us to go; and the remembrance of our early experience in Mexico made us dread renewed exposure to increased anxieties.

Every one was preparing for the exodus. Remates, escorts, and other details of travel were the common topics of conversation. One heard of little else than of the safest and most comfortable way of getting down to the coast. Bands of Liberals were said to be everywhere closing in upon the neighborhood; and although, of course, "diplomacy" had made the retreat of the French secure, some forethought must be exercised by travelers in order to insure safety on the journey.

January 2 was fixed upon as the most auspicious day for our departure. At this date the first detachment of the army was to be directed toward the coast, and we were to follow in its wake. Moreover, all along the road word had been sent to the military authorities to look after our safety in their respective jurisdictions, and everything was done to smooth our way.

For some evenings before our departure there was a round of simple festivities in the little colony. We were to leave first, but all must scatter soon. To me these entertainments seemed as lugubrious as a prolonged "wake." It was as though we were launching out in the night, and, like children in the dark, we sang aloud to keep up our courage.

For several days our patio rang with the clanging of swords, as our numerous military friends—I was about to say "comrades"—came to bid us Godspeed and to offer their services.

On our last night in Mexico a friend gave us a midnight supper, from which we were to step out at three o'clock in the morning to meet the stage which was ordered to stop and pick us up at the corner of the Paseo. This was intended to be a jolly send-off; only our nearest friends were asked. But what a mockery of mirth!

For three mortal hours we strove to affect what Henri Murger so wittily describes as the "gaiete de croque-mort qui s'enterre lui-meme"; and it was a relief when the moment came to make our last preparations.

The small party escorted us to the place where we were to board the coach. Oh, the gloom of that early start in the darkness of the morning! The dreariness of every one's attempt at cheerfulness! And then the approaching noise of the mules, and the rumbling of the wheels, as the somber mass neared the spot where we stood in weary expectancy. Exclamations of good will, kind wishes, a pressure of the hand, a last kiss, a farewell, a lump in the throat, a scurry, and a plunge into the dark hole open to receive us. At last the start, and, looking back, some whitish specks waving in the distance against the dark, receding group of friends left behind; and five years of my life, all the youth I ever knew, were turned down and closed forever! What was before me now?

We breakfasted at Rio Frio. Later in the day, at Buena Vista, between Puebla and the capital, we came upon a military encampment. It turned out to be the last remnant of the Belgian corps, then awaiting orders to proceed to the coast. As our stage halted, we had a few words with Colonel van der Smissen and other officers. There was in our party a Belgian captain who was on his way home. While chatting together, we saw at some distance, against a background formed by the Belgian camp, Princess Salm-Salm, in her gray-and-silver uniform, sitting her horse like a female centaur—truly a picturesque figure, with her white couvre-nuque glistening under the tropical sun.

The colonel had just received the intelligence that Maximilian, with his escort, would pass Buena Vista on the morrow, making his way to the capital.

Before we left Puebla, where General Douay was in command, we were told that the Emperor had started upon his journey to Mexico. He was escorted by a squadron of Austrian cavalry. A body of French Zouaves, which was to be relieved of duty upon his reaching the capital, was protecting the road. Besides the officers of his household, his physician, and his confessor, Father Pischer, Maximilian had with him General Marquez and his staff.

The prince was returning to the capital to prepare for the final struggle. He was determined to take his chances. These had been presented to him in as hopeful a light as the imagination of his interested councilors could place them. Now the time had come when he must arouse himself to action.

At Orizaba we learned that the Liberals were closing in at every point upon the ever-narrowing empire. The French having seized upon the Vera Cruz custom-house in payment of the war indemnity, the only source of supply was cut off, and the stress for money was terrible. The promise of financial relief mysteriously held out by the new cabinet had turned out to be delusive, and, it was soon found, was based upon the hope of a lottery! When the time for action came, the promised millions melted away, and all that the unfortunate monarch could scrape together, on the eve of entering upon a campaign on which hung his life, was a paltry fifty thousand dollars!

The troops were moving down. A large number of transports was waiting, and a fleet under Admiral la Ronciere le Noury was in readiness to escort the marshal and the army on the homeward journey.

Upon our arrival at Vera Cruz, we stopped at the Hotel de Diligencias to await the departure of the next outgoing vessel to New Orleans.

Here we were immediately called upon by Colonel Dupin, the commander of the region, who invited us to a breakfast to be given in our honor. He strongly impressed upon us the necessity of keeping indoors and avoiding exposure to the sun. This did not prevent our accepting an invitation to visit the Magenta, the flagship of Admiral Cloue, then in the harbor, upon hearing of which the colonel called again to remonstrate with us with regard to what he deemed an imprudence. Having been requested from headquarters to look after us, he regarded us as under his care, and evidently felt the burden of the responsibility.

Colonel Dupin was a picturesque figure. He was already an old man when I met him, and was regarded in the army as a brilliant officer of undaunted courage, but of questionable methods and of almost savage harshness.

He had taken part in the Chinese war, was present when the French and British allies entered Peking, and had a share in the sacking of the Summer Palace. He returned to France laden with a rich booty, including precious objects of artistic value, which he boldly exhibited for sale in Paris. This was against all military traditions, and in consequence Colonel Dupin's connection with the army was severed. Time had elapsed since this episode, however, and against Maximilian's expressed wishes he had been sent to Mexico by Napoleon himself to take command of the contre-guerilla formed for the defense of the coast region against the depredations of the Mexican bands. It was a relentless warfare, in which the vindictiveness of the Mexicans met with cruel reprisals. The most exaggerated stories were told of the brutality of the French commander, who, in order to intimidate the inhabitants, always in league with the guerrillas then infesting the region, treated them as accomplices whenever outbreaks occurred causing loss of life and property. This treatment, if it insured the submission of the people, was not likely to engender loyalty. Moreover, it earned for Colonel Dupin the title of "Tigre," of which, strange as it may appear, he seemed, I thought, rather proud.

The French army, with the marshal, made its final exit in state from the capital on February 5. At the last, and in order to insure their own safety, the French had surrendered the points held by them directly to the Liberal leaders.

Thanks to this prudent but unchivalrous policy,* the retreat of the army was as uneventful as had been the movement of concentration. The Liberal forces offered no opposition, and their guerrillas did not even harass the rear-guard of the retreating French. Several thousand men, mainly from the foreign legion, however, deserted. It is said that the marshal claimed them, but General Marquez replied that if he wanted them he might come and fetch them.

* Commandant Billaud was censured by his superior officers for having, in his retreat from Mexico to Puebla, beaten back a body of Liberal troops who had taken possession of the town of Chalco. See D'Hericault, loc. cit., p. 41.

On March 3 the marshal arrived in Vera Cruz with his last detachment, having lingered on the way, in the hope that the misguided Emperor might reconsider his decision and still be induced to join him. Orizaba and Cordoba were already in the hands of the Liberals, and all communication with the capital had virtually been cut off. The Commander-in-chief had not even heard of what had taken place since his departure.

Letters from members of the marshal's staff, received after we sailed from Vera Cruz, convey a graphic impression of the last days of the intervention.

From one under date of February 28, 1867, I quote the following passage:

Vera Cruz is overcrowded; many of the troops are on board their transports. The marshal is expected tomorrow. The Liberal army is already in Tacubaya, and bands are at Tacuba and all around the valley of Mexico ready to enter the capital. Every one thinks that the Emperor must leave very soon. Our orders are to hurry off our last detachments; perhaps we dread lest a cry for help should come from Mexico. Terrible confusion prevails here. Lodgings have given out, and officers sleep anywhere in the streets. Last night Vicomte de Noue slept on the staircase, having secured for his wife a room in which four beds were made for her, her three children, her two maids, her two dogs, and her three parrots! The price for such miserable accommodations is so exorbitant that everybody prefers going immediately on board. . . .

Another letter, dated March 4, says:

The marshal is as unpopular as ever with the army. His methods are censured by every one. The transports are here. With a better system our men might be shipped as soon as they arrive in this God-forsaken hole. Instead of this, however, unnecessary delay results in sickness among the rank and file. According to my orderly, who saw them, fifteen men were picked up this morning whom the surgeons had declined to embark. . . .

And the last, from another friend, under date of March 12, on board the Castiglione, says:

We sail to-day at eleven o'clock. For twenty-four hours out of Vera Cruz we are to form an escort to the Souverain, on board of which are the marshal and his wife, in order that their Excellencies may sail out of port in state. After this we will make straight for Toulon. All our men are at this moment on board their transports. The Mexican colors are flying over the citadel. The French intervention has come to a close, and is now a thing of the past. . . .

PART V

THE END

I. QUERETARO, 1867

The end is known. On February 13 the Emperor, with Generals Marquez and Vidaurri, at the head of a column of some two thousand men, sallied forth from Mexico to establish his base of operations at Queretaro.

After his defeat at San Jacinto (January 27), General Miramon, with the remains of his army, had fallen back upon Queretaro, then held by General Mejia with nine hundred men, and it was urged that Maximilian should there join his faithful generals. This plan, evolved by Senor Lares and the clerical leaders, had for its ostensible object to spare the capital the horrors of a siege. But it was more than suspected that a certain distrust had arisen between the Emperor and his Mexican supporters. They feared lest he also might make terms with the national party; and they wished, by inducing him to leave the capital, to put it out of his power to sacrifice them or their cause. Had he not once before, after accepting the crown at their hands, thrown himself into the arms of their enemies by calling Liberal leaders to his councils? However worthy in the eyes of posterity may appear Maximilian's attempt to reconcile opposing elements in the interest of peace and order, such a course was not calculated to inspire confidence in his personal loyalty to the once discarded extremists, now become his only supporters. Miramon and Marquez were not likely to forget that, in the hour of triumph of the monarchy erected by their hands, they had been sent, as wags then put it, one to study the art of fortification in Prussia, the other to watch the progress of civilization in Turkey.

It is difficult to penetrate all the hidden causes that governed the extraordinary policy followed at this time; but there is little doubt that individual interest and personal distrust played too large a part in its adoption. However this may be, it was at Queretaro that the last scene of the tragedy was enacted.

The auxiliary regiments, Maximilian's most trustworthy dependence in his extremity, were, by the advice of Marquez, left behind. The Emperor, he urged, must now throw himself entirely upon the Mexican nation. Thus Colonels Kodolitch, Khevenhuller, Hammerstein, and others, remained in Mexico, and only a few of the Emperor's foreign supporters followed him.

General Quiroga's division was withdrawn from San Luis and brought to Queretaro, while the veteran division of General Mendez, who had victoriously held Morelia and the Michoacan against the forces of Generals Regules and Corona, was likewise ordered, on February 13, to abandon that section of the country and to hasten to the Emperor's support. These leaders, with Generals Miramon, Marquez, Mejia, and Castillo, and General Arellano, who commanded the artillery, were the most conspicuous among the Imperialist officers gathered around Maximilian at this time.*

* A. Haus, "Queretaro: Souvenirs d'un Officier de l'Empereur Maximilien," pp. 11, 17.

During the cruel weeks of mingled hope and despair that had elapsed since he had left Chapultepec, Maximilian had conquered self. Now the ambitious Austrian prince, the weak tool of intriguing politicians, the upholder of religious and political retrogression, disappears; and where he had stood posterity will henceforth see only the noble son of the Hapsburgs, the well-bred gentleman who, aware of his failure, was ready to stand by it and to pay the extreme penalty of his errors.

Before the figure of Maximilian of Austria, from the time when he took command of his little army and resolved to stand for better or worse by those who had remained faithful to his fallen fortunes, all true-hearted men must bow with respect. From this time forth his words and acts were noble; and in his attitude at this supreme moment, his incapacity as a chief executive, his moral and intellectual limitations as a man, are overlooked. We forget that he was no leader when we see how well he could die.

It is noteworthy that, with the exception of General Miramon, those who had most urged upon him the last sacrifice were not with him to share it. Father Fischer disappeared from the stage of history almost as abruptly as he had entered it. Senior Lares and the cabinet, who were responsible for the last plan of action carried out by the Emperor, had remained in Mexico at the head of affairs. General Marquez, when the republican forces closed in upon the doomed empire, was sent from Queretaro with General Vidaurri, under an escort of cavalry led by General Quiroga, to raise supplies and reinforcements. He was vested with supreme authority as lieutenant of the empire, and had pledged himself to return with relief within twenty days. The Emperor wearily counted the hours as time went by; but, like the raven sent out from Noah's ark, General Marquez found enough to occupy him in the satisfaction of his own greed, and was never again heard from by him who sent him.

Overruling General Vidaurri, he deserted his imperial master in his extremity. He used the extraordinary powers given him to establish himself in the capital, where, for his own ends, he subjected the wretched inhabitants to the most cruel extortions. Routed at San Lorenzo* by General Diaz, who at once proceeded to besiege Mexico, he unduly prolonged the resistance of the city after the final downfall of the empire, exposing it to the unnecessary hardships of a four months' siege, the horrors of which were mitigated only by the generosity and forbearance of the Liberal commander.

* In the difficult retreat which followed these defeats, General Marquez fled with a body of two hundred cavalry, leaving his beaten army, then pursued by sixteen thousand men, to extricate itself as best it might. Colonel Kodolitch then assumed command, and fighting his way through the enemy, brought back the debris of the imperial forces, now reduced to one third, to the capital, where the general had preceded him.

It is said that this extraordinary conduct on the part of their official leader caused the indignant foreign officers no little concern with regard to the future. In order to guard against similar accidents, a council was held by the foreign leaders, Colonel Kodolitch, Captain von Wickemburg, Captain Hammerstein, Commanders Klickzing and Chenet, etc., who resolved that, although it was deeply humiliating for them to serve under a general who did not blush to desert his command under fire, as their service was needed by the Emperor they would retain their respective commissions; but in the moment of danger they would regard themselves as under the orders of Colonel Kodolitch. They further decided, should the city surrender, not to share in the terms of a Mexican capitulation, but to make their own terms, or, if necessary, to cut their way through to the sea.

See Charles d'Hericault, "Maximilien et le Mexique," page 231 et seq.

When at last the starving people rose in indignation, and would stand him no longer, he suddenly vanished. It is said that on the eve of being delivered into the hands of his enemies he managed his escape by concealing himself in a freshly dug grave. Twenty-seven years elapsed before the Mexican "Leopard" dared show his face once more in his native land, now transformed by the triumph of the men and of the institutions against which he had so desperately fought.

General Marquez, who, strangely enough, seems to have enjoyed the full confidence of his sovereign, had opposed with all his influence General Miramon's desire to conduct the war aggressively and to attack in detail the enemy's forces before they could unite to invest Queretaro.*

* A. Haus, loc. cit., page 164.

Gradually the republican divisions, arriving from all points of the country, were allowed to concentrate, until the imperial army was completely hemmed in. The heroic sorties with which the weary monotony of those weeks of expectancy was broken could now only result in the gradual exhaustion of the besieged and of their supplies. General Miramon, fretting under the restraint imposed upon him, saw the circle growing closer and stronger, until it was too late to make a winning fight. Only the energy of despair could contemplate a bare escape from the trap in which the Imperialists were now caught.

After a siege of over two months (from March 4 to May 15), during which his army had been cruelly depleted by frequent sorties and by the typhus fever now raging in the town, having abandoned all hope of relief from without, starvation staring him in the face, and ammunition beginning to fail, Maximilian and his still faithful generals resolved to cut their way through the enemy's lines with the little army, then numbering about nine thousand men and thirty-nine guns. This course had been urged for some time, but General Miramon, ever sanguine of ultimate success, had opposed the idea.

Three o'clock in the morning of May 14 was the time agreed upon for the sortie. Colonel Salm-Salm was to form a body-guard for the Emperor with the Khevenhuller hussars, the cavalry under Major Malburg, and the regiment of the Empress, commanded by Colonel Lopez.* All was in readiness. The gold and silver in the imperial treasury were divided for safe-keeping among four or five trusted men,** one of whom was Colonel Lopez, military commander of La Cruz, who enjoyed the confidence of Maximilian and had just received from him a decoration for valor.***

* Dr. Basch. (loc. cit., p. 229) mentions fifty of the Khevenhuller hussars, eventually increased to one hundred by volunteers, and eighty men were commanded by Major Malburg. Count Pacuta was lieutenant-colonel of the cavalry regiment of the Empress, of which Colonel Lopez was commander. These, led by Prince Salm-Salm, were to protect the Emperor during the sortie.

** Colonel Lopez, Colonel Pradillo, Colonel Campos, Colonel Salm-Salm, Dr. Basch, and the Emperor's secretary, Senor Blasio. See Basch, loc. cit., p. 233.

*** Colonel Lopez was highly thought of by the French, who had conferred upon him the red ribbon of the Legion of Honor. He was appointed to act on the imperial escort when the monarch landed, at Vera Cruz, and made himself agreeable to him. The dragoons of the Empress, of which he was the commander, were regarded as one of the best regiments in the army.

The man's political past, however, did not bear investigation, and when Maximilian, whose favorite he had become, thought of promoting him to the rank of general, the best among the officers of the imperial army requested General Mendez to inform the Emperor of his record. It has been stated that his disappointed hopes influenced his conduct in the dark transactions through which his name has been handed down to lasting infamy.

When the generals assembled in council at ten o'clock on the evening of May 13 to decide upon the final details of the projected sortie, General

Mejia stated that his preparations were not quite perfected, and it was decided to postpone the venture until the following night.*

* Salm-Salm, loc. cit.

At ten o'clock on the evening of May 14 the generals once more assembled in council of war with a view to arranging for the coming conflict; but again the execution of the project was postponed twenty-four hours.

It was past eleven o'clock when Colonel Lopez left the Emperor's room after talking over with his sovereign certain details connected with the service. Before he went out Maximilian asked him, should he be wounded in the sortie, to prevent his capture by blowing out his brains.*

* Basch, loc. cit., p. 233.

The Imperialist leaders had returned to their respective quarters. The Emperor, however, was ill with dysentery; the excitement of the approaching conflict kept him awake, and he did not retire till one o'clock. At 3 he was seized with violent pain, and sent for his physician. A profound stillness reigned over La Cruz as the doctor passed through its corridors, and no sign of the impending catastrophe attracted his attention.

But the angel of death was even then hovering over the group of brave men gathered within the walls of the old convent on that fateful night. The coming hours were pregnant with tragedy. At this very moment, destiny was at work ruthlessly clipping the threads of the web so painfully woven by them, and upon which hung their lives.

At 2 a. m. a young officer of artillery, Lieutenant Albert Haus,* to whose special care his superior officer had intrusted the handling of two pieces which, in the plan laid for the intended sortie, were to defend the entrance of the huerta, or garden, of La Cruz, was awakened, as previously arranged, by his old sergeant, as he slept, wrapped in his zarape, by the side of his battery.

* See "Queretaro: Souvenirs d'un Officier de l'Empereur Maximilien" (Paris, 1869).

For a while he paced up and down the platform, trying to overcome his drowsiness, as he took up his watch, and finally he sat down on one of the guns, feverishly awaiting the signal to prepare for the coming struggle; for he was unaware of any change in the orders given.

Suddenly he heard rapid footsteps coming toward him, and Colonel Lopez, recognizable in the dark by his uniform embroidered in silver, stood before him, followed at a short distance by a body of soldiers. Pointing to these, he said: "Here is a reinforcement of infantry. Arouse your artillerymen; have this gun taken out of its embrasure and turned obliquely to the left—quickly."

Believing that the time for the sortie had come, the lieutenant promptly called his men, while Colonel Lopez stood by impatiently, upbraiding in forcible terms the old sergeant, who, just aroused from his first sleep, was slow to obey. After repeating his orders, he hastily withdrew.

The lieutenant was surprised at the strange instructions given him, and although he reflected that the colonel must have good reasons for the command,—probably some cause to fear an attack on this point,—he instinctively felt a misgiving.

The platoon of infantry brought by Colonel Lopez had taken its stand behind the battery. After carrying out the colonel's orders, the lieutenant looked for his sword and his zarape, left by him on the ground where he had lain. They were missing. Suspecting the newcomers, he called their officer's attention to the fact. Then for the first time he noticed the strange demeanor of his new companions. The officer was utterly unknown to him. He seemed uncommunicative. There was something particularly unfamiliar in the men's appearance. Yet as a number of companies in the imperial army had been formed with city recruits or even with prisoners taken in the sorties during the siege, this alone would not have warranted serious suspicion. But when one of his artillerymen came up to him excitedly and complained that his musket had been taken from him, and when this complaint was promptly followed by another, he again went to the officer and inquired to what corps he and his men belonged. Without a moment's hesitation the stranger answered that he formed part of General Mendez's brigade.

Lieutenant Hans had long served in this brigade and knew all its officers. His doubts were at once aroused. The conviction gradually grew upon him that something unusual was taking place, and again he begged the officer to tell him the real cause of his presence at this post. The man answered that news had come that one of the battalions of the garrison of La Cruz had agreed to betray the place, but that fortunately the conspiracy had been discovered, and that all the posts were now being changed. This story tallied with the haste and peculiar manner of Colonel Lopez, the commander of the place, as well as with the unusual stir now visible farther along the line toward the pantheon. Anxious, however, to get at the truth, the lieutenant resolved to join the colonel, and asked the officer the direction which he had taken. The stranger silently pointed toward the pantheon.

As the lieutenant proceeded to descend from the terrace, a sentry, hitherto unnoticed, roughly stopped him, crying, "Halt, there!" The man evidently had his orders, and the lieutenant turned to the strange officer, requesting him to suspend them in his favor. The latter, however, evaded the question. This irritated him, and noticing just then a man holding one of the missing muskets, he attempted to tear it away from him, whereupon the soldier attacked him with his bayonet, and things might have gone hard with Lieutenant Haus had not the strange officer interfered.

"But," exclaimed the young man, "will you tell me what on earth is going on here?" "Do not worry," reiterated the strange officer." The truth is that we are part of General Quiroga's brigade. We have just returned from Mexico with General Marquez to relieve the place."

The palpable falsehood was enough to excite the young man's worst fears. General Quiroga, it was well known, had left his infantry at Queretaro. Moreover, it was quite impossible for troops to enter the closely besieged place without being heard and recognized by the besiegers. Something like the truth flashed through his brain. And yet how was he to account for the presence and words of Colonel Lopez, whose interest, as well as every tie of duty and gratitude, must bind him to the Emperor? In his bewilderment he exclaimed: "Amid so many falsehoods, I suspect treason." After a moment's hesitation the strange officer replied: "Have no fear, senor; you are in the hands of the regular army. We are not guerrilleros; we belong to the battalion of the supremos poderes of the republic."

For a moment the lieutenant stood petrified. The whole truth, in all its hideousness, burst upon him. The enemy was in possession of the place. What horrors would come next? And yet, Colonel Lopez—was it a hallucination? Could he have mistaken his identity in the darkness of the night? He called the old sergeant and asked him if he had recognized the colonel. "Yes," replied the sergeant, who, having been roughly handled by their superior officer, had good reason to remember.

"But then," cried the young man, beside himself, now that the terrors of the situation dawned upon his understanding, "he must be a traitor! He is going to deliver up the Emperor!"

"Are you only now finding this out?" sadly queried the old soldier.

Lieutenant Haus once more turned to the strange officer. "Then," he asked, "it is Colonel Lopez who introduced you here?"

"Certainly," he replied. And, smiling: "But, I repeat it, you need have no fear. We are of the regular army. No harm will come to you."

He looked toward La Cruz, the improvised stronghold where the Emperor had his headquarters, hoping to see some sign of a struggle—the flash of a musket, the noise of resistance, a movement, a signal. But no. The dark mass of the convent building detached itself with imposing grandeur against the night sky, and silence reigned everywhere.

He was a prisoner. The Juarists were in Queretaro, and treason even then was stealthily completing its loathsome task of destruction without his being able to give one word of warning to its victims.

The mysterious officer, guessing his thoughts, said quietly: "The whole convent is already in our power. Your emperor must be taken even now."

At this moment Captain Gontron, a Frenchman, appeared upon the scene, seemingly free, but in a towering rage.

"I wish," he said, "that you, who can speak Spanish better than I, would ask these black devils who have just come to relieve me at the pantheon why my sarape and my sword have disappeared. I believe they have stolen them. Anyhow, who are these filibusters that Colonel Lopez has brought here? If my sword does not turn up in five minutes, I will smash in the face of their rascally commander, who is anything but civil."

The captain spoke in French, fiercely twisting his mustache. At any other time the humorous side of the situation must have struck the lieutenant, but just then he felt little inclination for mirth. He thereupon explained to the captain that they were prisoners, and that Colonel Lopez had introduced the enemy into the place.

The Frenchman for a while stood speechless; then recovering his speech with his philosophy, he said: "After all, it had to come to an end SOMEHOW."

As he spoke, a Juarist officer, with a detachment at his heels, rushed upon the terrace and ordered a gun turned upon the convent. His orders were that the artillerymen be made to serve the battery. Should they demur, they must be shot down. As for the captain and the lieutenant, they were to be conducted under escort before General Velez, who was then in the convent. They were made to start at once.

Upon arriving near La Cruz, they saw a republican battalion entering the edifice. At every moment they expected to hear firing. But no one seemed aware of what was going on. Nothing broke the oppressive stillness save the dull sound of the tread of the enemy's detachments as they quietly marched along, and the quick orders whispered by the officers in the silence of the night.

Failing to find General Velez, the escort marched the prisoners back to the garden. Day was dawning. Upon reaching the garden they met Colonel Guzman, who had just been made prisoner.

The unusual incidents which had accompanied Colonel Lopez's betrayal had not remained wholly unobserved. It has been stated* that at 1:30 A.M. Colonel Tinajero, on watch at the convent heights, had come to headquarters and reported an unusual stir in the enemy's camp. The same writer adds that, later on, another officer had come to report that the Juarists seemed to be entering La Cruz.* He was laughed at for his pains. How could such a thing take place without a single shot being fired!

* By M. Charles d'Hericault, loc. cit, p. 252.

Colonel Manuel Guzman, a member of the Emperor's staff, however, thought it wise personally to look into the matter. He went down into the court of the convent, intending to visit the outposts. Here his progress was barred by the enemy. He was forthwith arrested and placed under the same escort as Lieutenant Haus and Captain Gontron, who, in a few words, told him what had happened. The colonel's face grew ashy. "Impossible!" he said; "what you tell me is impossible."*

* I here follow Lieutenant Haus's narrative, as it is based upon personal experience. Loc. cit., p. 284.

The prisoners now stood again upon the terrace which three hours before had been guarded by the men of the command of Colonel Jablonski, the friend and accomplice of Colonel Lopez. They were led across to the other side and made to pass down some hastily disposed steps of adobe bricks, the recent origin of which was obvious. It was clearly at this point that the enemy had entered the place. A few moments more, and they were out of Queretaro, marching between a double hedge of republican bayonets, disposed as though expecting a long line of prisoners.

At 5 A.M. Dr. Basch and Prince Salm-Salm were each abruptly startled out of a sound sleep, the first by Colonel Jablonski, the second by Colonel Lopez. Having completed their preparations beyond the possibility of failure, the traitors now wished, if practicable, to conceal from their victims their contemptible share in the dastardly affair.

Prince Salm-Salm dressed hastily, and after sending word by the doctor to Captain Furstenwarther to order out his hussars, he ran to the Emperor's apartments. No imperial troops were to be seen. It was evident that the garrison of the place had been removed.

As Maximilian, his minister, General Castillo, and his secretary came forth to inquire into what had happened, they found themselves face to face with the Liberal colonel Jose Rincon Gallardo, who, with his command, was already in possession of the place. With him was Colonel Lopez. The Liberal colonel recognized the fallen Emperor; but, perhaps foreseeing the terrible complications involved in his capture, he feigned ignorance of his identity, and said to his men, "Let them pass, they are civilians" ("Que passen, son paisanos"), thus giving him a chance for his life.

Shortly afterward, having reached the street, Maximilian was endeavoring, by issuing orders to his scattered officers, to collect his remaining forces on the Cerro de las Campanas, where he hoped to make a last stand, when he was joined by Colonel Lopez, whom, according to Prince Salm-Salm, no one as yet suspected of being the author of the infamy. The colonel had come to persuade the prince to conceal himself; and as they talked, his horse was unexpectedly brought to him, ready for flight. It would therefore seem that in betraying his master's cause the wretched man had not planned his personal destruction.

As the betrayed men continued their progress through the streets, on their way to the cerro, they saw coming toward them a battalion of the enemy; and among the officers riding at their head again was Colonel Lopez. Upon seeing the Emperor, they slackened their pace, and once more he was allowed to pursue his way.

Had he cared to avail himself of the opportunities afforded him then, it is possible that, like Generals Arellano, Gutierrez, and others, he might have succeeded in escaping from Queretaro. But noblesse oblige: an admiral does not desert his ship or its crew. Maximilian remained at his post.

At last the cerro was reached, and here the last disappointment awaited him. Instead of his army, only a battalion occupied the place, and, singly or in groups, the deserted leaders assembled, unable to rally their men.

General Mendez had accepted the shelter of a friend's roof. The latter, acting, it is said, in concert with a member of his staff, sold him to General Escobedo.*

* It was General Mendez who, in October, 1865, had carried out the provisions of the Bando Negro in executing Generals Salazar and Arteaga and their companions. He could therefore expect no mercy from his antagonists. He was condemned at once, and, as a traitor, was shot May 19, with his back to the four soldiers who carried out the sentence. Struck with four bullets, but not killed, the general arose, and turning to the men, begged that he be despatched. A corporal then stepped forward and mercifully blew out his brains. General Mendez was a courageous soldier. Always victorious, he was beloved by his men and was highly spoken of by the French in Mexico.

General Miramon, the man of action, always hopeful to the very last, was still attempting to muster what troops he might for a last effort, when at the corner of a street he unexpectedly was faced by a detachment of the enemy's cavalry. The commanding officer drew a revolver and shot him, the bullet entering the right cheek and coming out near his ear. The wounded chief then sought refuge in the house of a friend—who delivered him to his enemies that afternoon!

In the bright sunlight of the May morning there suddenly burst forth upon the air, already vibrating with the noise of the unequal conflict, a peal of bells from the convent of La Cruz. This was the signal of the success of the conspiracy, agreed upon with the besiegers; and from the lines of the Liberal army the clarions rang in wild, exultant strains. Then the dense masses of the enemy's regiments marched forth; and as they approached, the doomed leaders saw their own followers go over and join them.

Hemmed in upon the cerro with a few faithful followers, every hope passed away. No help came. It was now impossible, with so feeble a force, to cut their way through the lines of the Liberals, and from every side the enemy poured fire upon the devoted band.

A flag of truce was sent, and Colonel Echegaray, on behalf of the Juarists, came to receive the Emperor as prisoner. At the latter's request, he was taken forthwith to General Escobedo's presence. To him he surrendered his sword.

He was then turned over to General Riva-Palacio, who showed him every courtesy, and had him incarcerated in his old quarters at the convent of La Cruz. Here he was visited by some Liberal officers, among others by Colonel Jose Rincon Gallardo and his brother Don Pedro, the former of whom spoke to him in contemptuous terms of the treason of Colonel Lopez. "Such men are used, and then kicked," he said.

By ten o'clock all was over. The Mexican empire, inaugurated with so much pomp and glitter exactly three years before, had wearily reached a miserable ending. The curtain then falling upon its closing scene was a death-pall; and of the young sovereigns who only a short time before had regarded themselves as the anointed of Heaven, sent by a higher power to strengthen the church and to uphold the principles of monarchy, one had gone mad, and the other now stood an expiatory victim about to be offered up to republican resentment.

It would seem that Maximilian had at first no thought that his life was in peril. This is shown by his attempts to make terms with General Escobedo on behalf of his foreign followers, requesting that they and himself should be safely conducted to the coast and embarked; in exchange for which he pledged himself nevermore to interfere in Mexican affairs, and to issue orders for the disarmament and immediate surrender of all strongholds now in the power of his followers.

Soon, however, he was removed to the convent of the Capuchins, where he could be more securely guarded; and the feeling began to grow that he must pay with his life for his brief enjoyment of the Mexican crown.

Brought up for trial on June 13 before a military tribunal composed of six captains and one lieutenant-colonel, which held its court on the stage of a public theater, he was ably defended by Mexico's foremost lawyers, Messrs. Mariano Riva-Palacio, Martinez de la Torre, Eulalio Ortega, and Jesus-Maria Vazquez; but his doom was already sealed. On June 14, at eleven o'clock at night, he was sentenced to death.

Every effort was made by his lawyers and by the foreign representatives whom he had summoned to his side to obtain from the republican government a mitigation of the sentence. The Queen of England, the government of the United States, begged for mercy. Baron Magnus, Baron Lago, and M. de Hoorickx, in the names of the European monarchs allied to the prince by ties of relationship, moved heaven and earth to influence the president. Princess Salm-Salm cleverly used every means in a woman's power to accomplish the same end. In vain.

President Juarez could well afford to be magnanimous; but under the existing social conditions in Mexico, who, knowing all the facts, could blame if stern justice was allowed to take its course?

When Maximilian remained to carry on the civil war on factional lines, after the French, recognizing their mistake, had retired from the country, he placed himself, if taken, within the reach of the law. The people were then rising in arms, ready to drive out the empire. By his own act he deprived himself of the only excuse which he could logically offer for his presence in the country, namely, that in good faith he had accepted a crown offered him by what might be regarded as the suffrage of the nation, under conditions with the creating of which he had nothing to do. He was now only the factional leader of a turbulent and defeated minority.

Moreover, only a few months before, when General Miramon's brilliant coup de main of January 27, at Zacatecas, had come near to delivering into his hands the president of the republican government, Maximilian's instructions to his lieutenant, in anticipation of such a contingency, were to bring the republican leaders to trial, if caught, according to his too famous decree, but to refer the execution of the sentence to his imperial sanction. His official letter to this effect had fallen into the hands of President Juarez after the defeat of General Miramon at San Jacinto, which so speedily followed. It is open to doubt whether, in such an event, General Marquez, then all-powerful, would have allowed the Emperor to display mercy.

All hope of obtaining a commutation of the sentence now at an end, the energies of his friends, were turned toward effecting his escape. Three officers were bribed by Prince Salm-Salm, and steps were taken to provide the necessary disguise and conveyance for the party. The plan was to make for the Sierra Gorda, whence Tuzpan could be reached. From this point the party could proceed to Vera Cruz, then still holding out against the Juarists. The Austrian frigate Elizabeth, under Captain von Groeller, was at anchor in the port, awaiting the prince's pleasure.

The project had been seriously complicated by the positive refusal on the part of Maximilian to fly without Generals Miramon and Mejia. All details, however, were at last satisfactorily settled, and the night of June 2 was fixed for the attempt. On this night the officers whose good will had been secured were to be on guard, and the plot seemed easy of execution. But once more the innate in decision of Maximilian's character interfered. For some trivial cause he postponed the venture, and thus lost his last opportunity. Too many were in the secret for it to remain one. Some one made disclosures, which reached the ears of the authorities, and led to the complete isolation of the prince from his followers; and although another effort was afterward made, the surveillance was now so close, and the conditions had grown so difficult, that it also came to naught.

On June 15 tidings of the Empress Charlotte's death reached Queretaro. General Mejia, who was the first to hear it, broke it to Maximilian. While it stirred the very depths of his nature, this false information proved a help to him in his last moments. The bitterness of leaving his unfortunate wife in her helpless condition was thus spared him. "One tie less to bind me to the world," he said.

The execution had been fixed for June 16. At eleven o'clock on that day sentence was read to the condemned, who were told that it would be carried into effect at three o'clock on the same afternoon.

Maximilian received the intelligence calmly, and devoted the following hours, which he deemed his last, to dictating letters to Dr. Basch and to his Mexican secretary, Senor Blasio.* He then confessed to Padre Soria and heard mass in General Miramon's chamber, where the condemned men received the last sacraments, after which he signed his letters and took leave of those about him. In removing his wedding-ring and handing it to Dr. Basch, he said: "You will tell my mother that I did my duty as a soldier and died like a Christian." After this he quietly awaited death.

* One of these letters, written to Senor Don Carlos Rubio, reads as follows:

"Full of confidence, I come to you, being completely without money, to obtain the sum necessary for the carrying out of my last wishes. It will be returned to you by my European relatives, whom I have constituted my heirs.

"I wish my body taken back to Europe near that of the Empress; I intrust the details to my physician, Dr. Basch; you will supply him with funds for the embalming and transportation, and for the return of my servants to Europe. The settlement of the loan will be made by my relatives either through any

European house that you may name or by drafts sent to Mexico. The physician above alluded to will make all necessary arrangements.

"Thanking you in advance for any favor, I send you farewell greetings, and wishing you happiness,

"I am yours,
"Maximilian."
"Queretaro, 16 June, 1867."

Compare S. Basch, "Maximilien au Mexique," p. 296.

The appointed hour passed, however, without being summoned to execution. After prolonged suspense, at four o'clock in the afternoon news arrived that a reprieve of three days had been granted by the president, in order that the condemned might make their last dispositions.

{illustration caption: THE CALVARY OF QUERETARO, SHOWING WHERE MAXIMILIAN, MEJIA, AND MIRAMON WERE SHOT.}

This unexpected delay* naturally aroused hopes among the friends of the doomed men. These hopes, it is said by those closest to him at that time, were not shared by Maximilian. He continued his preparations with the calm dignity that had not once forsaken him; but he sent a telegram to the national government, asking that the lives of Generals Miramon and Mejia, "who had already undergone all the anguish of death, be spared," and that he might be the only victim. The request was denied.**

*It is stated by Domenech that this reprieve was granted at the request of Baron Magnus, who hoped that delay might bring some chance of life to the condemned.

** He also wrote to President Juarez, under date of June 19, as follows:

"M. Benito Juarez: About to die for having tried whether new institutions could put an end to the bloody war which has for so many years disturbed this unhappy land, I should gladly give my life if the sacrifice could contribute to the peace and prosperity of my adopted country. Profoundly convinced that nothing durable can be produced from a soil drenched with blood and shaken by violence, I pray you solemnly—with that sincerity peculiar to the hour at which I have arrived—I beg of you, let my blood be the last spilled, and pursue the noble course which you have chosen with the perseverance (I recognized it even when in prosperity) with which you defended the cause that now at last triumphs through your efforts. Reconcile factions, establish a durable peace based upon solid principles."

See Dr. Basch, "Maximilien au Mexique," p. 303.

After making this supreme effort on behalf of his generals, he employed his remaining hours in dictating letters, and when night came he slept soundly.

On the morning of his execution (June 19) he arose at three o'clock, and dressed carefully. At four o'clock Padre Soria came, and once more gave him the last sacraments; an altar had been erected for this purpose in a niche formed by a passageway to his cell.

This religious duty having been performed, he gave instructions to Dr. Basch, sending greetings and last tokens to friends. At a quarter before six he breakfasted; and when, on the stroke of six, the officer appeared who was to lead him to execution, he was ready, and himself called his companions in death. Three hacks had been provided for the condemned. The prince entered the first with the priest, and, escorted by the soldiery, the mournful procession moved through a dense crowd to the place of execution.

On arriving at the Cerro de las Campanas, where a month before he had made his last stand, the fallen Emperor looked about him for a friendly face, and finding only his servant, the Hungarian Tudos, he asked, "Is no one else here?" It is said, however, that Baron Magnus, the Prussian minister, and the Consul Bahnsen were present, although out of sight.

{illustration caption: THE HACK IN WHICH MAXIMILIAN WAS TAKEN TO THE PLACE OF EXECUTION.}

The good priest weakened under the ordeal; he felt faint, and the prince held his own smelling-bottle to his nose.

Followed by Generals Miramon and Mejia, Maximilian walked toward the open square, where an adobe wall had been erected, against which they were expected to stand. About to take his position in the middle, Maximilian stopped, and turning to General Miramon, said: "A brave soldier should be honored even in his last hour; permit me to give you the place of honor"; and he made way for him.

An officer and seven men had been detailed to do the deadly work. The prince gave each of the soldiers a piece of gold, asking them to aim carefully at his heart; and taking off his hat, he said: "Mexicans, may my blood be the last to be spilled for the welfare of the country; and if it should be necessary that its sons should still shed theirs, may it flow for its good, but never by treason. Long live independence! Long live Mexico!"*

* "Que me sangre sea la ultima que se derrame en sacrificio a la patria; y si fuese necessario algunos de sus hijos, sea para el bien de la nacion, y nunca en traicion de ella." Other versions of his last words have been given, but that given above seems the most authentic, not only from intrinsic

probability, but from the fact that it was given, shortly after the execution, by the Mexican Dr. Reyes, who was present, to Dr. Basch. Loc. cit., p. 308.

He then laid his hands on his breast, and looked straight before him. Five shots fired at short range pierced his body; each of them was mortal. He fell, and as he still moved, the officer in charge pointed to his heart with his sword, and a soldier stepped, forward and fired a last shot.

The physician who afterward examined the remains, preparatory to embalmment, could not find a single bullet; all had gone through the body, and it was his opinion that death must have been almost instantaneous, and that the movements observed were convulsive.*

* Dr. Basch says: "The head was free from wounds. Of the six shots received in the body, three had struck the abdomen, and three the breast almost in a straight line. The shots were fired at shortest range, and the six bullets so perforated the body that not a single one was found.

"The three wounds in the chest were mortal: one had reached the heart, the two ventricles; the second had cut the great arteries; the third had gone through the right lung. From the nature of the wounds the death-struggle must have been very brief, and the poetic words attributed to the Emperor, giving anew the word of command to 'fire,' could not have been pronounced. The motions of his hands must have been the convulsive motions which, according to physiological laws, accompany death caused by sudden hemorrhage."

The bodies of the two generals were given to their families. That of Maximilian, inclosed in a common coffin, was placed in the chapel of the convent of the Capuchins, and delivered up to the doctor.

As President Juarez insisted upon an official request, made in due form by the Austrian government, before delivering the remains, much delay occurred in the carrying out of the unfortunate prince's wishes with regard to them.

At last, on November 1, the coffin containing the body of Ferdinand Maximilian Joseph, Archduke of Austria, Prince of Hungary and Bohemia, Count of Hapsburg, Prince of Lorraine, Emperor of Mexico, was handed over to Admiral Tegetthoff, who had been sent on a special mission to receive it, and left the capital with a cortege composed of his staff and an escort of one hundred cavalry.

On November 26 the Novara, with all that remained of the Emperor, left the Mexican shore, where only three years before he had landed in all the pride of power and the hopefulness of ambitious youth. The news of his execution sent a painful thrill through the civilized world. By one of those r cruel ironies which fate seems to affect, it reached France on the day of the formal distribution of prizes at the International Exposition. Paris, in its splendor, was throwing open its gates to all the nations of the earth; the crowned heads and leaders of Europe had accepted the hospitality of Napoleon III; and all outward appearances combined to make this the most brilliant occasion of his reign. But the flash-light and noise of French fireworks were unable to drown in men's hearts the dull echo of those distant shots fired on the Cerro de las Campanas. Nemesis was near, and only a short time after Queretaro, Sedan, Metz, and Chiselhurst were inscribed in gloomy sequence upon the pages of history.

APPENDIX A

THE BANDO NEGRO (BLACK DECREE) PROCLAMATION OF EMPEROR MAXIMILIAN, OCTOBER 3, 1866

Mexicans: The cause sustained by D. Benito Juarez with so much valor and constancy had already succumbed, not only before the national will, but before the very law invoked by him in support of his claims. To-day this cause, having degenerated into a faction, is abandoned by the fact of the removal of its leaders from the country's territory.

The national government has long been indulgent, and has lavished its clemency in order that men led astray or ignorant of the true condition of things might still unite with the majority of the nation and return to the path of duty. The desired result has been obtained. Men of honor have rallied around the flag and have accepted the just and liberal principles which guide its policy. Disorder is now only kept up by a few leaders swayed by their unpatriotic passions, by demoralized individuals unable to rise to the height of political principle, and by an unruly soldiery such as ever remains the last and sad vestige of civil wars.

Henceforth the struggle must be between the honorable men of the nation and bands of brigands and evil-doers. The time for indulgence has gone by: it would only encourage the despotism of bands of incendiaries, of thieves, of highwaymen, and of murderers of old men and defenseless women.

The government, strong in its power, will henceforth be inflexible in meting out punishment when the laws of civilization, humanity, or morality demand it.

Mexico, October 2, 1885.

Maximilian, Emperor of Mexico: Our Council of Ministers and our Council of State having been heard, we decree:

Article I. All individuals forming a part of armed bands or bodies existing without legal authority, whether or not proclaiming a political pretext, whatever the number of those forming such band, or its organization, character, and denomination, shall be judged militarily by the courts martial. If found guilty, even though only of the fact of belonging to an armed band, they shall be condemned to capital punishment, and the sentence shall be executed within twenty-four hours.

Article II. Those who, forming part of the bands mentioned in the above article, shall have been taken prisoners in combat shall be judged by the officer commanding the force into the power of which they have fallen. It shall become the duty of said officer within the twenty-four hours following to institute an inquest, hearing the accused in his own behalf. Upon this inquest a report shall be drawn and sentence shall be passed. The pain of death shall be pronounced against offenders even if only found guilty of belonging to an armed band. The chief shall have the sentence carried into execution within twenty-four hours,—being careful to secure to the condemned spiritual aid,—after which he will address the report to the Minister of War.

Article III. Sentence of death shall not be imposed upon those who, although forming part of a band, can prove that they were coerced into its ranks, or upon those who, without belonging to a band, are accidentally found there.

Article IV. If from the inquest mentioned in Article II facts should appear calculated to induce the chief to believe that the accused has been enrolled by force, or that, although forming part of the band, he was there accidentally, he shall abstain from pronouncing a sentence, and will consign the prisoner, with the corresponding report, to the court martial, to be judged in accordance with Article I.

Article V. There shall be judged and sentenced under the terms of Article I of the present law:

I. All individuals who voluntarily have procured money or any other succor to guerrilleros.

II. Those who have given them advice, news, or counsel.

III. Those who voluntarily and with knowledge of the position of said guerrilleros have sold them or procured for them arms, horses, ammunition, provisions, or any other materials of war.

Article VI. There shall be judged and sentenced in accordance with Article I:

I. Those who have entertained with guerrilleros relations constituting the fact of connivance.

II. Those who of their own free will and knowingly have given them shelter in their houses or on their estate.

III. Those who have spread orally or in writing false or alarming news calculated to disturb order, or who have made any demonstration against the public peace.

IV. The owners or agents of rural property who have not at once given notice to the nearest authority of the passage of a band upon their estate.

The persons included in the first and second sections of this article shall be liable to an imprisonment of from six months to two years, or from one to three years' hard labor, according to the gravity of the offense.

Those who, placed in the second category, are connected with the individual concealed by them by ties of relationship, whether as parents, consorts, or brothers, shall not be liable to the penalty above prescribed, but they shall be subject to surveillance by the authorities during such time as may be prescribed by the court martial.

Those included in the third category shall be sentenced to a fine of from twenty-five to one thousand piasters or to one year's imprisonment, according to the gravity of the offense.

Article VII. When the authorities have not given notice to their immediate superior of the passage of an armed force in their locality, the superior authority shall inflict a fine of from two hundred to two thousand piasters or from three months' to two years' imprisonment.

Article VIII. Every inhabitant who, having knowledge of the passage of an armed band in a village or of its approach, has not notified the authorities shall be liable to a fine of from five to five hundred piasters.

Article IX. All inhabitants between the ages of eighteen and fifty-five years of age not physically incapacitated shall, when the locality inhabited by them is threatened by a band, take part in the defense of the place, under penalty of a fine of from five to two hundred piasters or of from fifteen days' to four months' imprisonment. If the authorities deem it proper to punish the village for non-resistance, they may impose a fine of from two hundred to two thousand piasters, which shall be payable by all those who have not taken part in the defense.

Article X. The owners or agents of country property who, being able to defend themselves, have not kept guerrillas and other evil-doers away from their estates or have not notified the nearest military authority of their presence, or who have received the tired or wounded horses of the guerrillas without advising the said authority, shall be punished by said authority by a fine of from one hundred to two thousand piasters, according to the gravity of the offense. In cases of extreme gravity they shall be arrested and brought before the court martial, to be judged in conformity with the rules laid down by the present law. The fine shall be paid to the principal administrator of the revenue of the district where the estate is situated. The provisions of the first part of the present article are applicable to the populations.

Article XI. All authorities, whether political, military, or municipal, who have not acted in accordance with the provisions of the present law against those who are suspected of or recognized as being guilty of the offenses with which it deals, shall be liable to a fine of from fifty to one thousand piasters; and when the omission implies acquaintance with the guilty, the delinquent shall be brought before the court martial, who shall judge him and inflict a penalty in proportion to the offense.

Article XII. Plagiarios* shall be judged and sentenced under the provisions of Article I of the present law, without regard to the circumstances under which the abduction shall have been committed.

* Kidnappers.

Article XIII. Sentence of death passed upon those guilty of the offenses enumerated by the present law shall be executed in the time fixed, and the benefit of appeal for mercy shall be refused to the condemned. When the accused has not been condemned to death, and is a stranger, the government, after he shall have undergone punishment, may make use with regard to him of its right to expel from its territory pernicious strangers.

Article XIV. Amnesty is proclaimed in favor of all who, having belonged or still belonging to armed bands and having committed no other offense, shall present themselves to the authorities before the 10th of next November. The authorities shall take possession of the arms of those so surrendering themselves.

Article XV. The government reserves unto itself the right to fix the time when the provisions of the present law shall cease to be enforced. Each of our ministers is bound, as far as his department is concerned, to enforce the present law and to issue such orders as will secure its strict observance.

Issued in the Palace of Mexico, October 3, 1865.
Maximilian.

The Minister of Foreign Affairs, intrusted with the Department of State, Jose F. Ramirez.

The Minister of Commerce, Luis Robles Pezuela.

The Minister of the Interior, Jose Maria Esteva.

The Minister of War, Juan de Dios Peza.

The Minister of Justice, Pedro Escudero y Echanove.

The Minister of Public Instruction and of Cults, Manuel Siliceo.

The Under-Secretary of the Treasury, Francisco de P. Cesar.

APPENDIX B

TREATY OF MIRAMAR, SIGNED ON APRIL 10, 1864

Napoleon, by the grace of God and the national will Emperor of the French, to all who will see the present letters, Greeting:

A convention, followed by secret additional articles, having been concluded on April 10,1864, between France and Mexico, to settle the conditions of the sojourn of French troops in Mexico, the said convention and secret additional articles are as follows:

The government of H. M. the Emperor of the French and that of H. M. the Emperor of Mexico, animated with. an equal desire to assure the reestablishment of order in Mexico and to consolidate the new empire, have resolved to settle through a convention the conditions of the sojourn of the French troops in that country, and have appointed to that effect: H. M. the Emperor of the French, M. Charles Francois Edouard Herbet, Minister Plenipotentiary of the First Class, etc., and H. M. the Emperor of Mexico, M. Joaquin Velazquez de Leon, his Minister of State without a portfolio, etc., who, after communicating their full powers to one another, these having been found to be in good and due form, have agreed upon the following articles:

Article I. The French troops actually in Mexico shall, as soon as possible, be reduced to a corps of twenty-five thousand men, including the foreign legion. This corps, as a safeguard to the interests which have brought about the French intervention, shall temporarily remain in Mexico under the conditions agreed upon in the following articles.

Article II. The French troops shall gradually evacuate Mexico as H. M. the Emperor of Mexico shall be able to organize the troops necessary to take their place.

Article III. The foreign legion in the service of France, composed of eight thousand men, shall, however, remain for six years in Mexico after all other French forces shall have been recalled under Article II. From that date said legion shall pass into the service and pay of the Mexican government, the Mexican government reserving unto itself the right to shorten the duration of the employment in Mexico of the foreign legion.

Article IV. The points of the territory to be occupied by the French troops, as well as the military expeditions of said troops if necessary, shall be determined under direct agreement between H. M. the Emperor of Mexico and the Commander-in-chief of the French corps.

Article V. Upon all points where a garrison shall not be exclusively composed of Mexican troops, the military command shall devolve upon the French commander. In case of combined expeditions of French and Mexican troops the superior command shall also belong to the French commander.

Article VI. The French commanders shall not interfere with any branch of the Mexican administration.

Article VII. So long as the needs of the French army-corps will require every two months a service of transports between France and the port of Vera Cruz, the expense of this service, fixed at the sum of four hundred thousand francs per journey, including return, shall be borne by the Mexican government and paid in Mexico.

Article VIII. The naval stations supported by France in the Antilles and in the Pacific Ocean shall frequently send ships to show the French flag in the Mexican ports.

Article IX. The cost of the French expedition in Mexico, to be reimbursed by the Mexican government, is fixed at the sum of two hundred and seventy million francs from the time of the expedition to July 1, 1864. That sum shall bear interest at three per cent. a year.

Article X. The indemnity to be paid to France by the Mexican government for the pay and support of the army-corps from July 1, 1864, shall be fixed at the rate of one thousand francs per man a year.

Article XI. The Mexican government shall at once remit to the French government the sum of sixty-six millions in loan securities at par, i.e., fifty-four millions to be deducted from the debt mentioned in Article IX, and twelve millions as an instalment on the indemnities due the French under Article XIV of the present agreement.

Article XII. In payment of the balance of war expenses and of the charges mentioned in Articles VII, X, and XIV, the Mexican government agrees to pay to France the annual sum of twenty-five million francs in cash. That sum shall be credited, first, to the sums due under Articles VII and X, second, to the amount, interest and principal, of the sum fixed in Article IX; third, to the indemnities still due to French subjects under Article XIV and following.

Article XIII. The Mexican government shall pay on the last day of every month, in Mexico, into the hands of the paymaster-general of the army, the amount necessary to cover the expense of the French troops remaining in Mexico, in conformity with Article X.

Article XIV. The Mexican government agrees to indemnify French subjects for the grievances unduly suffered by them and which caused the expedition.

Article XV. A mixed commission composed of three Frenchmen and three Mexicans, appointed by their respective governments, shall meet in Mexico within three months to examine into and settle these claims.

Article XVI. A mission of revision composed of two Frenchmen and two Mexicans, appointed as above and sitting in Paris, shall proceed to the definite settlement of the claims already admitted by the commission mentioned in the preceding article, and shall pass upon those the settlement of which shall be reserved to them.

Article XVII. The French government shall set free all Mexican prisoners of war as soon as H. M, the Emperor of Mexico shall have entered his empire.

Article XVIII. The present convention shall be ratified and the ratification shall be exchanged as soon as possible.

Done at the Castle of Miramar, on April 10, 1864.
Herbet. Velazquez.

Additional Secret Articles

[Here follow the ordinary preambles.]

Article I. H. M. the Emperor of Mexico, approving the principles and promises announced in General Forey's proclamation, dated June 12, 1863, as well as the measures taken by the regency and by the French general-in-chief in accordance with said declaration, has resolved to inform his people, by a manifesto, of his intentions in the matter.

Article II. On his side, H. M. the Emperor of the French declares that the actual effective force of the French corps of thirty-eight thousand men shall only be reduced gradually and from year to year, in such a way that the French troops remaining in Mexico, including the foreign legion, shall be of twenty-eight thousand men in 1865, of twenty-five thousand in 1866, of twenty thousand in 1867.

Article III. When the said foreign legion, under the terms of Article III of the above convention, shall pass into the service and pay of Mexico, as it nevertheless shall continue to serve a cause in which France is interested, its generals and officers shall preserve their quality of Frenchmen and their claim to promotion in the French army according to law.

Done at the Castle of Miramar, on April 10, 1864.
Herbet. Velazquez.

CPSIA information can be obtained
at www.ICGtesting.com
Printed in the USA
LVHW031738010323
740520LV00003B/817

9 789356 896451